NOBU THE SUSHI BOOK

Nobu Matsuhisa

SEKAIBUNKASHA INC.

MEASUREMENTS

This book follows the standard North American system of volume measurements (cup, tablespoon, teaspoon) rather than the weight system (kg, gm) preferred in the UK and Europe. Japanese home and professional cooks use a mixture of both volume and weight, depending on the ingredient. Metric measures are noted in parentheses.

1 cup = 240 ml
1 tablespoon = 15 ml
1 teaspoon = 5 ml
1 ounce = 30 grams

1 inch = 2.5 cm
3 teaspoons = 1 tablespoon
16 tablespoons = 1 cup

EDITOR AND TRANSLATOR'S NOTE

Editing and translating a cookbook is exciting, but challenging work; it is both a tremendous opportunity and yet a great responsibility. Because there is no single system that everyone agrees upon for transcribing Japanese into English, there are many choices, and that becomes a boon and a burden.

Whenever possible I chose to use English terms rather than Japanese: soy sauce, not *shōyu*; lotus root, not *rénkon*. When that does not work, I borrow Japanese to describe English in the main text and provided a fuller explanation in the glossary: *akagai* clam; énoki mushroom are examples. Sometimes I had to reverse the order, borrowing English to describe Japanese: box-pressed sushi; red miso. Often there is no simple English, and lengthy explanations become clumsy. That's when I let Japanese words stand alone, explaining them on the same page; unwieldy explanations were placed in the glossary. To help you pronounce unfamiliar words, I have used accent marks ō, ū, é.

When Japanese words are awkwardly long, I break them into logical segments: *tamagoyakinabé*, a Japanese omelet pan, was broken into *tamagoyaki* (omelet) and *nabé* (pan). Sometimes a compound word is the best solution, and I use a hyphen to show when pronunciation changes: pressed (*oshi*) sushi, becomes *oshi-zushi*: the "s" of "sushi" changes to a "z."

I have striven to be true to Nobu's original work, which so brilliantly shows his many faces: creative culinary force, generous and gracious teacher, diligent professional. His motto is the importance of "*kokoro*," a word that translates as "heart" but really describes an attitude of care that shines through all he does. I hope I have enabled you to benefit from his abundant talents.

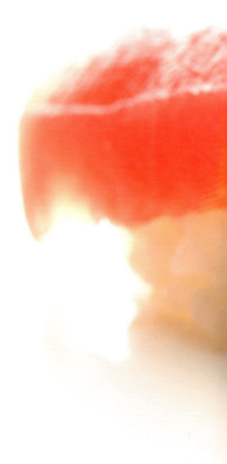

Published by Sekaibunkasha Inc.,
4-2-29 Kudan-kita, Chiyoda-ku, Tokyo 102-8187, Japan.

©2025 Nobuyuki Matsuhisa

All rights reserved. Printed in Japan.
ISBN 978-4-418-25309-8

www.sekaibunka.com

CONTENTS

Editor and Translator's Note   4
Introduction   6
Essential Sushi Ingredients   8
Sushi Rice   12
Buying and Handling Fish   14
Essential Sushi Equipment   15

Sushi Rolls   16

NOBU Hand Roll Sushi Party Box   50

Nigiri Sushi   54

Home Entertaining Sushi Party Ideas   94

Sushi Bowls & Box-Pressed Sushi   98

NOBU-Style Soups   112

Appetizer Sushi   118

Saké and Aperitifs   134

Sushi Course Dishes   140

Classic Techniques   148
NOBU Sauces for Sushi   151
Basic Seafood Preparation for Sushi   153
About the Chef and the Restaurants   161
NOBU in the World   164
Glossary   165
Index   170

INTRODUCTION
THE MAGIC OF SUSHI

"REALLY GOOD NIGIRI SUSHI"

Because each nigiri sushi is caringly formed by hand, a layer of soft air is captured between the grains of rice. When set down on a plate, the sushi should settle, ever so slightly, with its own weight. That's the precise moment at which to place the sushi in your mouth. In an instant, the rice releases its sweetness and mingles with the lively flavor of the seafood. Really good sushi is all about that magic moment: knowing it, seizing it, savoring it.

"SUSHI IS SIMPLE, YET TRICKY."

It's easy to press too hard when forming nigiri sushi or shaping sushi rolls. If you do, the rice gets crushed, making it too hard or sticky to enjoy. Sushi rice served *chirashi*-style, in bowls, also must be handled very gently, tossing, not mashing, when mixing it with condiments. Sushi is not about forcing food to take shape; it's about taking care, and caring deeply.

"*KOKORO*, COOKING FROM THE HEART, IS MY MOTTO."

The recipes in this book are written for all who want to try making sushi on their own. I have included both traditional and NOBU-Style sushi dishes. I've tried to instruct you as best I can with step-by-step photos and detailed descriptions of techniques and ingredients. But learning to make good sushi is not easy. You will need to practice; keep trying until you get the knack of it. Improving your skills in the kitchen is important.

Fine food is made from the heart. Perhaps that is the most important lesson.

"SUSHI DEFINES ME. IT IS WHO I AM, WHAT I DO."

I began cooking professionally at the age of 18, in the late sixties. My first position was as an apprentice at Matsuei Zushi, in Tokyo's Shinjuku district. Thereafter I journeyed to Peru, then to Argentina and the United States in pursuit of a grand dream: to share with the world the glories of Japan's food and food culture. Today, I own restaurants in 13 countries that span the globe, and yet my dream remains unchanged. Each time I prepare sushi for a guest at one of my restaurants, I am reminded of this. Sushi has become my way of sharing my appreciation for Japan's marvelous food and culinary traditions with an international audience. While my cooking has no doubt been influenced by North and South American food ways, it is still deeply Japanese. And, sushi is at the core.

Nobuyuki Matsuhisa

ESSENTIAL SUSHI INGREDIENTS

While sushi requires solid technique, at its core it is a simple cuisine, all the more reason to use the best-quality ingredients possible. Aside from the toppings and fillings, following are the essential ingredients for making sushi at home.

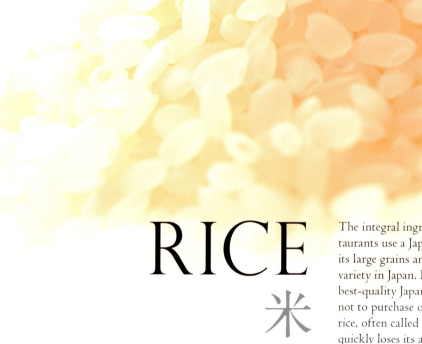

RICE 米

The integral ingredient for sushi is rice. All of the NOBU restaurants use a Japanese variety called *koshihikari*. Renowned for its large grains and rich flavor, *koshihikari* is the most popular variety in Japan. If you cannot find *koshihikari*, look for the best-quality Japanese variety of short-grain rice. (Be careful not to purchase opaque *mochigomé*, which is a different type of rice, often called sticky rice, glutinous rice, or sweet rice.) Rice quickly loses its aroma and flavor after it is milled and polished, so try to source freshly polished rice.

Wash the rice in a bowl with water and promptly rinse several times until the water runs clear. Since dry rice grains rapidly soak up water, it is important to wash and rinse with fresh water quickly (see details on PAGE 12). After the rice is cooked, incorporate the Seasoned Vinegar (PAGE 12) until each grain has a glossy sheen.

NORI

海苔

Nori is essential for making sushi rolls and *gunkan* sushi (PAGE 93). Look for high-quality toasted and unseasoned nori that is crisp and has the rich fragrance of the sea. Nori will lose its delicate aroma and signature texture if it becomes damp, so store it in a dry place or buy it in small batches.

A full sheet of nori measures a generous 8 × scant 8 inches (21 × 19 cm). Most of the sushi rolls at NOBU are made from half sheets of nori. Each full sheet is cut in half lengthwise, each half sheet measuring generous 4 × scant 8 inches (10.5 × 19 cm). When rolling sushi, be sure to put the shiny side down and have the rough side of the nori facing up. That way the shiny side is on the outside of the roll.

RICE VINEGAR 酢

Rice vinegar is a key component in making sushi. Good rice vinegar should be round on the palate and have a lively acidity. NOBU uses a red rice vinegar made from saké rice lees that is rich and refreshing. When making the Seasoned Vinegar (PAGE 12) for sushi rice, combine sugar, salt, mirin, and kombu with the rice vinegar and cook. NOBU's special technique is to add some uncooked rice vinegar to the cooked mixture to give it a fresh aroma.

SUGAR 砂糖

NOBU uses a highly refined granulated sugar to add a refreshing sweetness to the sushi rice. As with the salt, be sure that the sugar dissolves when making the Seasoned Vinegar.

SALT 塩

Salt is used for its salinity and for its ability to draw out flavors. NOBU uses a coarse Japanese sea salt. Be sure that the salt dissolves in the Seasoned Vinegar so that it will be fully incorporated into the rice.

KOMBU 昆布

Rich in glutamic acid, kombu kelp adds natural umami to the seafood, vegetables, and sushi rice. There are four major varieties of kombu available in the market. At NOBU the high-glutamate Rausu kombu is preferred. See glossary (PAGE 169).

MIRIN 味醂

Known as sweet rice wine, mirin adds not only a rich flavor and sweetness but also a luster to the sushi rice, even if only a small amount is added to the Seasoned Vinegar. See glossary (PAGE 169).

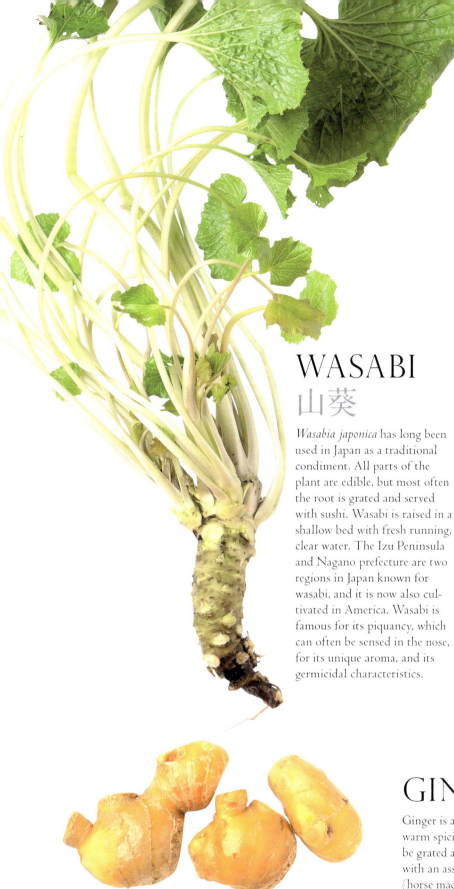

WASABI
山葵

Wasabia japonica has long been used in Japan as a traditional condiment. All parts of the plant are edible, but most often the root is grated and served with sushi. Wasabi is raised in a shallow bed with fresh running, clear water. The Izu Peninsula and Nagano prefecture are two regions in Japan known for wasabi, and it is now also cultivated in America. Wasabi is famous for its piquancy, which can often be sensed in the nose, for its unique aroma, and its germicidal characteristics.

Traditionally fresh wasabi is grated on a sharkskin grater. The dried sharkskin has a gentle yet rough texture that is ideal for finely grating the fibers of the wasabi root into a thin paste. Look for a fat and moist root, peel the thin layer of the outer skin and grate by using a circular motion to bring out its notable aroma and spicy flavor. Wasabi root loses its aroma quickly after it is grated, so it is best to grate in small batches. Alternatively, look for good-quality, processed fresh wasabi. Kinjirushi makes various wasabi products.
www.kinjirushi.co.jp/english/

GINGER 生姜

Ginger is a condiment with a notable aroma and a warm spiciness. After peeling the thin skin, it can be grated as a garnish, in place of wasabi, for fish with an assertive flavor such as mackerel and *aji* (horse mackerel). Look for aromatic fresh ginger that is juicy and has tender fibers.

SUSHI RICE

MAKES ABOUT 7 CUPS

3 cups (720 ml) short-grain rice, preferably Japanese

3 cups (720 ml) water

Seasoned Vinegar

⅔ cup (160 ml) red rice vinegar or regular rice vinegar (PAGE 10)

4 teaspoons salt

½ cup (100 grams) granulated sugar

scant 1 tablespoon mirin

2-inch (5 cm) square sheet kombu

WASHING THE RICE:

Place the rice in a large bowl and cover with plenty of cold water. Vigorously stir and rinse the rice with your hand. The water will become very cloudy with starch. Drain the rice in a fine-mesh strainer. Return the rice to the bowl and add ample cold water. Gently stir the rice so as not to break the grains. Drain the rice when the water becomes cloudy. Repeat this washing procedure a few times, until the rinsing water is almost clear. Return the washed rice to the bowl, cover with ample cold water, and soak for 20 to 30 minutes. The rice will become slightly opaque as the grains absorb water.

COOKING THE RICE:

Drain and transfer the rice to the bowl of an electric rice cooker. Add measured water, cover, and cook. If you want to cook rice on a stovetop, place the rice in a large and sturdy pot with measured water. Cover the pot with a tight-fitting lid. Place the pot over high heat and bring the water to a boil. When you hear bubbling sounds or see steam escaping, reduce the heat to low and continue to cook for 15 minutes. It is best not to open the lid during this cooking process. Remove from heat, still tightly covered, and let stand for another 10 minutes.

TO MAKE SUSHI RICE:

1. Reserve 3 tablespoons of vinegar. Combine the remaining ingredients for Seasoned Vinegar in a saucepan and bring to a boil over high heat. Turn off the heat after the granulated sugar dissolves and remove the kombu. After it has cooled to room temperature, mix in the reserved vinegar. This ensures the fresh flavor of the Seasoned Vinegar. Thoroughly wipe the inner surface of the *handai* wooden rice tub (PAGE 15) with a cloth that is dampened with vinegar water. If a *handai* is not available, substitute a large plastic container with a flat bottom. The plastic container does not need to be dampened with vinegar water.

2. Transfer the warm rice to the *handai* and pour the Seasoned Vinegar over the rice.

3. Use gentle cutting and folding motions with a *shamoji* (PAGE 15) or a spatula, incorporate the Seasoned Vinegar into all of the rice. Doing it quickly prevents the rice from getting too sticky.

4. Spread the rice into a thin even layer on the bottom of the *handai*. Take special care not to break or crush the grains.

5. In order to cool the rice, scoop up a small amount, turn it over, and place it back at the same spot. Repeat this process, scooping and turning over the rice little by little.

6. Smooth out the rice surface with the *shamoji*. Cover with a lid or with a damp cloth until used to prevent it from drying.

BUYING AND HANDLING FISH

This book is about sushi, and so it calls for fresh fish and seafood on nearly every page. It is important that you buy only sashimi-grade product (food that is safe to consume raw) from a reliable source. It is equally important that you practice excellent kitchen hygiene:

- To prevent cross-contamination, designate a special cutting board just for sushi and sashimi; wash it thoroughly and be sure to dry it completely after each use.
- Refrigerate immediately and consume everything the day of your purchase. Work swiftly but carefully to ensure the fish remains in good condition.
- Once the sushi is made, serve and enjoy it quickly.
- If there is leftover fish or seafood, refrigerate and cook it the following day: Do NOT eat leftover sushi or sashimi raw.

CUTTING FISH FILLETS

(Instructions are written for right-handed people. Reverse if you are left-handed.)

For making sushi with fish, you might be lucky enough to find pre-cut sashimi pieces available at your nearby grocery store or Japanese supermarket, sometimes in the freezer section. It's best to get sashimi-grade fish fillets (often in *saku* form: fillets that are trimmed in a rectangular shape, which is ideal for producing evenly cut pieces of fish) and slice the fish just before serving, since pre-cut sashimi pieces can dry quickly.

For most sushi rolls, the fish fillet is cut into long strips. For most nigiri sushi and sushi bowls, the fillet is cut diagonally to produce a thin and even rectangular slice. This is called the *sogi-giri* cutting technique. First place the fillet on a cutting board in a horizontal position, lightly press the left end of the fillet with your left fingers, and insert the blade of your knife at an appropriate angle just underneath your left fingers. Gently work the knife through the fillet to yield a slice.

When it comes to nigiri sushi, each fish slice ideally measures about 3 × 1 inch (7.5 × 2.5 cm) and ¼ inch (5–6 mm) thick (PHOTO 1), and weighs a scant ½ ounce (12–15 grams). A fish slice of this size when topped on a well-balanced portion of sushi rice becomes a perfect mouthful of nigiri sushi. Since the fillets vary in size, shape, and thickness, you should think carefully how your knife is angled when cutting slices.

Here is an example. Looking at PHOTO 2, if you work from the head end of the flounder fillet, your knife should be placed almost vertically to the fillet to allow a slice to be 3 inches (7.5 cm) long, and the knife is also held at about a 45-degree angle to make the slice 1 inch (2.5 cm) wide. When you work from the tail end of the fillet (PHOTO 3), which is narrower and thinner, your knife is placed more horizontally and at an angle to the fillet axis in order to ensure that uniform slices are cut.

A FEW MORE TIPS FROM THE PRO ABOUT SLICING FISH FILLETS:

—Professional (right-handed) sushi chefs use their left fingers to measure out the nigiri slices from the fillets. The width of four fingers, from index finger to little finger, is about 3 inches (7.5 cm), and one and a half times the width of the index finger measures about 1 inch (2.5 cm) (PHOTO 1).

—Tuna and salmon often have tough sinews, so it is better to cut the fillet across the sinews, not parallel to them, so that you don't encounter their toughness when you eat the fish (PHOTO 4).

—White lean fish such as sea bream, sea bass, and flounder has a generally chewy texture and is better when sliced slightly thinner than the full-flavored tender fish such as tuna, salmon, and yellowtail (PHOTO 5).

ESSENTIAL SUSHI EQUIPMENT

The equipment essential for making sushi can be found at specialty kitchenware stores, at Asian supermarkets, and online.

HANDAI AND SHAMOJI

A *handai*, also known as *sushi oké* or *hangiri*, is a large, flat-bottomed tub, and a *shamoji* is a rice paddle. These are used for dressing cooked rice with seasoned vinegar. The *handai* is usually made of cedar or cypress, which absorbs the excess moisture from the sushi rice mixture and prevents it from getting mushy. Moisten a clean cloth with vinegar water and wipe the *shamoji* and interior of the *handai* before using. Put the cooked rice in the *handai*, add the seasoned vinegar, and use the *shamoji* to toss. Be sure to thoroughly clean the *handai* and *shamoji* after each use and dry them completely. If they are not dried well, they may become infected with mold.

MAKISU

A *makisu* is a flexible mat woven of bamboo splints used to roll nori and rice around fillings. Moisten a clean cloth with vinegar water and squeeze tightly, then wipe the *makisu* before using. If the *makisu* has a smooth and a rough side, the smooth side should face up. If the warp threads have a fringe, it should be set further from you. The rice may stick to the *makisu* when making an inside-out roll, so wrap the *makisu* with plastic wrap before using. Be sure to wash and dry thoroughly to prevent it from being infected with mold.

JAPANESE KNIVES

High-quality Japanese knives are made of carbon steel and are only sharpened on one side of the blade, normally on the right side for right-handed users. To maintain the knife's super-sharp edge and to prevent it from rusting, the knife needs to be kept dry and sharpened with a whetstone frequently, or have it done professionally. Japanese knives should never be put in a dishwasher or ever sharpened with a steel knife sharpener.

The following two knives, along with an *usuba-bōchō* (PHOTO: PAGE 152) which has a thin rectangular blade and is used to peel and cut vegetables, can do most of the tasks for making sushi.

LEFT: *Yanagiba-bōchō*. This long, narrow blade resembles a willow leaf *(yanagiba)* and is used exclusively for slicing boneless fish fillets. The whole of the blade is used when cutting: start at the end nearest you and pull the knife towards you in one long cut.
RIGHT: *Déba-bōchō*. This blade is thick and heavy, making it ideal for working with fish and meat. Smaller fish require a smaller *déba-bōchō*.

15

SUSHI ROLLS

Maki-Zushi

Sushi rolls are nori that is topped with sushi rice, layered with fillings, and rolled. With a rich history in Japan, now it is not surprising to find this traditional Japanese food with a variety of fillings around the world.

There are 5 kinds of sushi rolls at NOBU: plump rolls, thin rolls, inside-out rolls, thick rolls, and hand rolls. Following are the basics for making sushi rolls step-by-step, complete with detailed photos and recipes for a variety of popular rolls. Many of the NOBU-Style rolls have become the standard around the world.

HOUSE SPECIAL ROLL (see PAGE 18 for recipe) »

PLUMP ROLLS

HOUSE SPECIAL ROLL

The most popular fillings for sushi rolls in America are tuna, salmon, and *hamachi* yellowtail, all of which are included in this sushi roll. This recipe also includes popular snow crab legs and avocado for a succulent roll.

MAKES 1 ROLL; 6 PIECES

⅔ cup (120 grams) sushi rice

½ sheet nori

4 strips sashimi-grade tuna, salmon, *hamachi* yellowtail, and white-fleshed fish such as sea bass (*suzuki*), sea bream (*tai*), or flounder (*hiramé*), each ½ inch (1 cm) thick and 4 inches (10 cm) long

meat of 1 boiled snow crab leg, cut into 4-inch (10-cm) lengths

1 avocado wedge, cut lengthwise

1 tablespoon chopped scallions or chives

1 tablespoon *masago* roe

grated wasabi

4×12-inch (10.5×30-cm) *katsuramuki* sheet of roseheart radish (or daikon, carrot, or cucumber) (PAGE 19)

soy sauce for dipping

BASIC TECHNIQUE FOR ROLLING A PLUMP ROLL:

1 Lay the *makisu* on your work surface with the splints crosswise. If the *makisu* has a smooth and a rough side, the smooth side should face up. Place the nori lengthwise, shiny side down, close to the lower edge of the *makisu*.

2 Dip both hands in ice-cold water and shake off any excess. Form a log of the sushi rice and place on the nori one-third of the way from the top.

3 With damp fingertips, evenly spread the sushi rice toward you, making sure not to crush the grains.

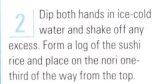

4 Spread the rice just up to the left and right edges of the nori without spilling over. One hand can spread the rice while the other hand prevents the rice from spilling over the edges.

5 Leave a generous 1-inch (3-cm) strip uncovered at the farther edge and a ½-inch (1-cm) strip at the closer edge. Align the edge of the nori along the closer edge of the *makisu*.

6 Spread some wasabi across the center of the rice. Next scatter the scallions and spread the *masago* roe. Arrange all of the fish and avocado pieces on the rice as shown.

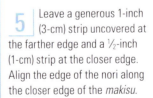

PLUMP ROLLS

7 Placing your thumbs under the *makisu* and holding the fillings with the remaining fingers, lift up the lower edge of the *makisu*.

8 Roll the *makisu* tightly, wrapping the rice and nori around the fillings. The nori strip at the upper edge should still be visible. Gently draw the *makisu* towards you with four fingers to tighten and shape the roll.

9 Pick up the *makisu* and push the roll forward until it is fully covered with nori.

10 Cover the roll with the *makisu* again and gently press the whole roll.

11 Place the roll on the trimmed sheet of *katsuramuki* roseheart radish and wrap.

12 Cut the radish-covered roll into 6 pieces with a sharp knife, wiping the blade with a damp cloth after each cut. Serve with soy sauce.

NOBU-STYLE 1

WRAPPING THE SUSHI ROLL IN A VEGETABLE *KATSURAMUKI*.

Many of NOBU's rolls are wrapped in a broad, paper-thin sheet of raw vegetable *katsuramuki* made from daikon, cucumber, or other root vegetables. This vegetable wrapping originated in the eighties, when many diners were not yet accustomed to nori. The natural color of the vegetable is appealing, and the crunch creates an elegant and delicious roll. Please be extra careful, as this is a very difficult technique and could be dangerous.

BASIC *KATSURAMUKI* TECHNIQUE

(Instructions are written for right-handed people. Reverse if you are left-handed.)

1 Cut off a generous 4-inch (10- to 11-cm) segment from a fresh daikon. Preferably cut a part near the middle, somewhat closer to the bottom, because this is juicy and tender enough to work with.

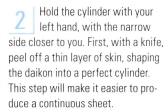

2 Hold the cylinder with your left hand, with the narrow side closer to you. First, with a knife, peel off a thin layer of skin, shaping the daikon into a perfect cylinder. This step will make it easier to produce a continuous sheet.

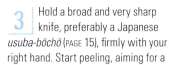

3 Hold a broad and very sharp knife, preferably a Japanese *usuba-bōchō* (PAGE 15), firmly with your right hand. Start peeling, aiming for a broad, paper-thin continuous sheet. Place your left thumb close to the cutting edge, where it can guide the cutting, move the blade up-and-down (forward and backward) in a sawing motion to cut smoothly and evenly. At the same time, your left hand should turn the daikon slowly as the blade moves.

4 From the continuous sheet, trim 4×12-inch (10.5×30-cm) sheets for the outer layer of plump rolls. Lightly rinse with cold water, roll up, cover with plastic wrap, and refrigerate until used. This will keep for 2 days.

19

SOFT-SHELL CRAB ROLL

SALMON SKIN ROLL

SOFT-SHELL CRAB ROLL

Deep-fried soft-shell crab is rolled and served while the crab is still hot in this signature NOBU roll. The crisp shell of the fried crab is a bright contrast to the juicy meat.

MAKES 1 ROLL; 6 PIECES

⅔ cup (120 grams) sushi rice

½ sheet nori

1 fresh raw soft-shell crab, generous 4 ounces (130 grams)

katakuriko (potato starch) or cornstarch

oil for deep-frying

1 tablespoon chopped scallions or chives

1 tablespoon *masago* roe

1 avocado wedge, cut lengthwise

4×12-inch (10.5×30-cm) *katsuramuki* cucumber sheet (PAGE 19)

soy sauce for dipping

Wash the soft-shell crab and blot dry with a paper towel. Dust with *katakuriko*. Be sure to thoroughly dust the inside of the carapace and the legs of the crab.

    Heat the oil in a deep skillet or a deep-fryer to 350°F (180°C) and submerge the soft-shell crab. After 1 minute turn over. When the sputtering sound becomes clearer, transfer to a wire rack on a cooking tray to drain. Leave for about 5 minutes on the rack, and it will become a little soggy and moist. Deep-fry a second time at 350°F (180°C) for about 3 minutes. The crab should be crisp on the outside and juicy inside. Cut the crab in half down the middle.

    Lay the nori on the *makisu* lengthwise, shiny side down. Dampen both hands with ice-cold water and form the sushi rice into a log. Place it on the nori and spread out evenly. Scatter chopped scallions and spread *masago* roe. Arrange avocado and put both crab halves on top, while they are still warm and crisp. Flatten the crab a little and roll up.

    Wrap the roll with the *katsuramuki* cucumber sheet and cut into 6 pieces. Serve with soy sauce. See instructions under House Special Roll (PAGE 18).

SALMON SKIN ROLL

The skin of smoked salmon is rich with umami and has just the right amount of salt, which makes a nice match with the creamy avocado and tart/sweet sushi rice.

MAKES 1 ROLL; 6 PIECES

⅔ cup (120 grams) sushi rice

½ sheet nori

2×5-inch (5×13-cm) piece (1 ounce/30 grams) smoked salmon skin

smoked salmon to taste — if the skin doesn't have much flesh attached

1 tablespoon olive oil

2 green *shiso* leaves

1 avocado wedge, cut lengthwise

1 pickled burdock root, store-bought (PAGE 169)

kaiwaré daikon sprouts

1 tablespoon chopped scallions or chives

1 teaspoon toasted white sesame seeds

itogaki (dried bonito threads)

4×12-inch (10.5×30-cm) *katsuramuki* carrot sheet (PAGE 19)

soy sauce for dipping

Heat the olive oil in a frying pan over medium heat and add the salmon skin, skin side down. Press down with a spatula until the fat melts and the skin is brown and crisp. Flip over and remove from the pan immediately when the color of the flesh changes. Cut into ¼-inch (5-6 mm) strips. Sauté and flake the smoked salmon meat (optional).

    Lay the nori on the *makisu* lengthwise, shiny side down. Dampen both hands with ice-cold water and form the sushi rice into a log. Place it on the nori and spread out evenly. Scatter chopped scallions and sesame seeds. Arrange the *shiso* leaves, avocado, pickled burdock root, *kaiwaré* daikon sprouts, fried salmon skin, flaked salmon, and *itogaki* on the rice and roll up.

    Wrap the roll with the *katsuramuki* carrot sheet and cut into 6 pieces. Serve with soy sauce. See instructions under House Special Roll (PAGE 18).

NOTE

If it is hard to find salmon skin, try to get a large piece of smoked salmon with skin attached and cut the skin from the filet.

 PLUMP ROLLS

VEGETABLE ROLL

Popular not only with vegetarians, this refreshing roll with vegetables is a hit with many. Offering a variety of textures and flavors, this roll is anything but monotonous. The presentation of the cut roll is also beautiful and fun.

MAKES 1 ROLL; 6 PIECES

⅔ cup (120 grams) sushi rice

½ sheet nori

1 green *shiso* leaf

kaiwaré daikon sprouts

1 to 2 okra pods, stemmed and sepals removed

½ to 1 stalk asparagus, blanched in salted water, cut into generous 4-inch (10-cm) lengths, and halved lengthwise if too thick

1 to 2 thin cucumber sticks, cut into generous 4-inch (10-cm) lengths

1 pickled burdock root (store-bought, PAGE 169), cut into generous 4-inch (10-cm) lengths

1 avocado wedge, cut lengthwise

1 tablespoon chopped scallions or chives

1 teaspoon toasted white sesame seeds

4×12-inch (10.5×30-cm) *katsuramuki* yellow or regular carrot sheet (PAGE 19)

soy sauce for dipping

Lay the nori on the *makisu* lengthwise, shiny side down. Dampen both hands with ice-cold water and form the sushi rice into a log. Place it on the nori and spread out evenly. Scatter the chopped scallions and sesame seeds over the rice. Arrange the green *shiso* leaf, *kaiwaré* daikon sprouts, okra, blanched asparagus, cucumber, pickled burdock root, and avocado and roll up.

    Wrap the roll with the *katsuramuki* yellow carrot sheet and cut into 6 pieces. Serve with soy sauce. See instructions under House Special Roll (PAGE 18).

TORO ROSSA ROLL

What appears to be Korean barbecue beef is actually medium-fatty tuna (*chūtoro*). When the fat tuna is seared lightly, it emits its aromas and umami. Once rolled, enjoy immediately while the tuna is still warm and its rich flavor is at its peak.

MAKES 1 ROLL; 6 PIECES

⅔ cup (120 grams) sushi rice

½ sheet nori

2 slices sashimi-grade medium-fatty tuna (*chūtoro*)

2 tablespoons Garlic Soy Sauce (PAGE 151)

1 tablespoon chopped scallions or chives

1 to 2 leaves frilly leaf lettuce, such as red leaf lettuce

5 to 6 pieces Crispy Garlic Chips (see BELOW)

2-inch (5-cm) length Japanese leek (*naganégi*)

kaiwaré daikon sprouts

1 tablespoon Spicy Saikyō Miso Sauce (PAGE 151)

4×12-inch (10.5×30-cm) *katsuramuki* daikon sheet (PAGE 19)

Crispy Garlic Chips: Peel and slice one or two garlic bulbs. Heat oil in a deep skillet or a deep-fryer to 210°F (100°C) and add garlic slices. Slowly bring up the temperature to 360°F (180°C); it should take about 5 minutes to come to temperature, stirring frequently. Just before the chips turn brown, remove from oil and spread on a paper towel to cool.

Score the leek lengthwise. Remove and discard the light green core. Finely shred the leek along the fiber and soak in cold water for 2 to 3 minutes. Drain and blot dry.

Lay the nori on the *makisu* lengthwise, shiny side down. Dampen both hands with ice-cold water. Form the sushi rice into a log. Place it on the nori and spread out evenly. Scatter the chopped scallions. Add the frilly lettuce, Crispy Garlic Chips, leek shreds, and *kaiwaré* daikon sprouts with the stems inside and the leaves outward.

Preheat a *yakiami* grill (PAGE 165). Place Garlic Soy Sauce in a bowl. Add the tuna to the bowl to quickly marinate in the sauce, then sear for 5 seconds on each side. Place the seared tuna on the frilly lettuce. Add Spicy Saikyō Miso Sauce and roll.

Wrap the roll with the *katsuramuki* daikon sheet and cut into 6 pieces. See instructions under House Special Roll (PAGE 18).

NOTE

With a *yakiami* grill, you can sear fish over a direct flame on the stove top. See GLOSSARY.

THIN ROLLS

NEW STYLE SASHIMI ROLL

Listen for the sound of the hot sesame oil searing the sashimi and take in the aroma of the *yuzu* as it blossoms. This is a thin roll with the classic NOBU New Style Sashimi.

MAKES 1 ROLL; 6 BITE-SIZED PIECES

generous ⅓ cup (70 grams) sushi rice

½ sheet nori

3 slices sashimi-grade sea bass (*suzuki*)

⅛ teaspoon finely grated garlic

a few chives, cut into 2-inch (5-cm) lengths

1 small piece fresh ginger, peeled, finely julienned, soaked in cold water, and blotted dry (*hari shōga;* "needle-cut ginger")

1 teaspoon toasted white sesame seeds

1 tablespoon Yuzu Soy Sauce (PAGE 151)

2 teaspoons New Style Oil (PAGE 151)

soy sauce for dipping

PREPARATION:
Arrange the sea bass slices on a plate in one layer and lightly spread grated garlic on each piece. Top with chive pieces, julienned ginger, and sesame seeds. Drizzle Yuzu Soy Sauce over the fish.

Heat New Style Oil in a pan until it just starts to smoke. Pour over the sea bass. It should sizzle and become fragrant.

BASIC TECHNIQUE FOR ROLLING A THIN ROLL:

1. Lay the nori on the *makisu* crosswise, shiny side down. Dampen both hands with ice-cold water. Form the sushi rice into a log, and place it on the nori.

2. Spread the rice to the left and right edges without spilling over, leaving a scant 1-inch (2-cm) strip uncovered at the upper edge and a scant ½-inch (1-cm) strip at the lower edge. Arrange the seared sea bass slices and aromatics on top of the rice while they are still warm. Thin rolls are tricky to roll and can easily rupture, so be careful not to fill it with too many ingredients.

3. Lift up the lower edge of the *makisu* and roll tightly, wrapping the rice and nori around the fillings. Gently draw the roll towards you with four fingers to tighten and shape it.

4. Pick up the *makisu* and push the roll forward until it is fully covered with the nori.

5. Cover the roll with the *makisu* again and gently press the whole roll. Cut the roll into 6 pieces with a sharp knife, wiping the blade with a damp cloth after each cut. Serve with soy sauce.

NOBU-STYLE 2

NEW STYLE SASHIMI

Arrange fresh sashimi with chives, julienned ginger, and Yuzu Soy Sauce before pouring over the smoking hot oil; listen for the sizzling sound. Just the outside of the sashimi is cooked, leaving the inside raw, which gives it a lively flavor and unique texture. The aromas of the herbs and sauce are accentuated by the hot oil. This method is good for those who are not yet enamored of raw seafood and was created as a way to help those diners cross that bridge. Not only with white fish, this preparation is good with salmon, scallops, squid, and oysters. (All should be sashimi-grade.) Add some asparagus or other vegetables, and your repertoire of sushi rolls increases with this New Style Sashimi technique.

SALT-PRESERVED CUCUMBER ROLL

YELLOWTAIL AND JALAPEÑO ROLL

TUNA AND ASPARAGUS ROLL

THIN ROLLS

YELLOWTAIL AND JALAPEÑO ROLL

Spicy jalapeño is the perfect accent for the rich *hamachi* yellowtail.

MAKES 1 ROLL;
6 BITE-SIZED PIECES

generous ⅓ cup (70 grams) sushi rice
½ sheet nori
1 strip sashimi-grade *hamachi* yellowtail, ½ inch (1 cm) thick, 8 inches (21 cm) long
½ jalapeño chili, top trimmed off, seeded, and thinly sliced
10 coriander leaves
soy sauce for dipping

Lay the nori on the *makisu* crosswise, shiny side down. Dampen both hands with ice-cold water. Form the sushi rice into a log. Place it on the nori and spread out evenly. Arrange the *hamachi* yellowtail, jalapeño chili, and coriander leaves on the rice. Roll and cut into 6 pieces. Serve with soy sauce. See instructions under New Style Sashimi Roll (PAGE 26).

SALT-WILTED CUCUMBER ROLL

The texture of the crisp, salted cucumber is balanced with the aromatic and flavorful *myōga*.

MAKES 1 ROLL;
6 BITE-SIZED PIECES

generous ⅓ cup (70 grams) sushi rice
½ sheet nori
1 Salt-Wilted Cucumber
½ *myōga* bud, cut in half lengthwise
1 teaspoon toasted white sesame seeds
grated wasabi

To make Salt-Wilted Cucumber: Bury Japanese cucumbers in a bed of salt and refrigerate for about 1 month. The salt is replaced a couple of times as liquid is released from the cucumbers and the salt bath becomes too wet. Salt-Wilted Cucumbers can be stored in the salt in the refrigerator for another month.

Just before using, soak the Salt-Wilted Cucumber in cold water for 10 minutes to reduce the salinity. Remove from water, squeeze to remove excess water, and slice into thin rounds. Cut the *myōga* bud into thin slices lengthwise and soak in cold water for 2 to 3 minutes. Drain and blot dry.

Lay the nori on the *makisu* crosswise, shiny side down. Dampen both hands with ice-cold water. Form the sushi rice into a log. Place it on the nori and spread out evenly. Spread some wasabi across the center of the rice. Arrange the sliced cucumber and *myōga*, and scatter sesame seeds. Roll up and cut into 6 pieces. See instructions under New Style Sashimi Roll (PAGE 26).

TUNA AND ASPARAGUS ROLL

Tuna and asparagus are paired with Avocado Mayonnaise Sauce to make a rich and luscious roll.

MAKES 1 ROLL;
6 BITE-SIZED PIECES

generous ⅓ cup (70 grams) sushi rice
½ sheet nori
1 strip sashimi-grade tuna, ½ inch (1 cm) thick, 8 inches (21 cm) long
½ to 1 stalk asparagus, blanched in salted water, cut into generous 8-inch (21-cm) lengths, and cut in half lengthwise if too thick
2 teaspoons Avocado Mayonnaise Sauce (PAGE 151)
grated wasabi
soy sauce for dipping

Lay the nori on the *makisu* crosswise, shiny side down. Dampen both hands with ice-cold water. Form the sushi rice into a log. Place it on some nori and spread out evenly. Spread some wasabi across the center of the rice. Arrange the tuna and asparagus on the rice. Pipe Avocado Mayonnaise Sauce along the tuna. Roll and cut into 6 pieces. Serve with soy sauce. See instructions under New Style Sashimi Roll (PAGE 26).

INSIDE-OUT ROLLS

CALIFORNIA ROLL

The invention of the inside-out roll came in the 1980s in California as a way to serve sushi by putting the sushi rice on the outside and disguising the nori inside. Avocado and crab meat were alternatives for diners who were still getting used to eating raw seafood. After 30 years in existence, the California Roll is now popular throughout the world and also at NOBU restaurants worldwide.

MAKES 1 ROLL;
6 BITE-SIZED PIECES

½ cup (100 grams) sushi rice
½ sheet nori
2 avocado wedges, cut lengthwise
meat of 2 boiled snow crab legs
2 thin cucumber sticks, 4 inches (10 cm) long
grated wasabi
1 to 2 teaspoons toasted white sesame seeds
soy sauce for dipping

BASIC TECHNIQUE FOR ROLLING AN INSIDE-OUT ROLL:

1 Fully cover the *makisu* with plastic wrap with the seam underneath the makisu. Lay the nori on the *makisu* crosswise, shiny side down. Dampen both hands with ice-cold water and form the sushi rice into a log. Place it on the nori.

2 Spread the rice to the left and right edges without spilling over, leaving a scant ½-inch (1-cm) strip uncovered at the upper edge but slightly extending beyond the nori at the lower edge. Scatter sesame seeds evenly over the rice.

3 Pinch the lower edge of the nori with both fingers and flip over forward so that the nori is on top. Spread some wasabi across the center of the nori, and arrange the avocado, crabmeat, and cucumber.

4 Before rolling, pull down the nori to align it along the lower edge of the *makisu*. Placing your thumbs under the *makisu* and holding the fillings with the remaining fingers, lift up the lower edge of *makisu* and roll.

5 Pick up the *makisu* and push the roll forward until the rice and nori fully wrap around the fillings.

6 Cover the roll with the *makisu* again and gently press the whole roll. Cut the roll into 6 pieces with a sharp knife, wiping the blade with a damp cloth after each cut. Serve with soy sauce.

INSIDE-OUT ROLLS

SHRIMP TEMPURA ROLL

Crunchy shrimp tempura, crisp boiled asparagus, and creamy Spicy Mayonnaise Sauce go well together in this popular roll.

MAKES 1 ROLL; 6 BITE-SIZED PIECES

½ cup (100 grams) sushi rice

½ sheet nori

2 fresh black tiger shrimp, head and shell attached

Tempura Batter
> 1 cup (100 grams) cake flour or all-purpose flour
> 1 egg, chilled
> generous ¾ cup (200 ml) cold water

1 to 2 stalks asparagus, blanched in salted water, cut into 8-inch (21-cm) lengths, and halved lengthwise if too thick

2 teaspoons Spicy Mayonnaise Sauce (PAGE 151)

1 to 2 teaspoons toasted white sesame seeds

oil for deep-frying

soy sauce for dipping

Tempura Batter: Beat the egg with water in a bowl. Add the flour and lightly stir with a whisk. Do not overmix. The batter should still have some lumps. Refrigerate until ready to use.

To make the shrimp easy to roll, it is essential to straighten it before deep-frying. First remove the head, peel, and devein the shrimp. Score across the belly side three times and flatten the shrimp by pressing down on its back with a finger (PHOTO 1). Using a brush, lightly and evenly dust with flour as needed.

Heat the oil in a deep skillet or a deep-fryer to 340°F (170°C). Dip flour-dusted shrimp in the cold Tempura Batter (PHOTO 2). Deep-fry in the oil for about 3 minutes until crisp (PHOTO 3).

Lay the nori crosswise on the plastic-covered *makisu,* shiny side down. Dampen both hands with ice-cold water, form the sushi rice into a log, and place it on the nori. Spread the rice evenly, leaving a scant ½-inch (1-cm) strip uncovered at the upper edge but slightly extending beyond the nori at the lower edge. Scatter sesame seeds evenly over the rice. Pinch the lower edge of the nori with both fingers and flip over forward so that the nori is on top.

Place the shrimp tempura on the nori while still warm and crisp. Arrange the asparagus and Spicy Mayonnaise Sauce along the shrimp. Roll and cut into 6 pieces. Serve with soy sauce. See instructions under California Roll (PAGE 31).

INSIDE-OUT ROLLS

SPICY ROLLS

Popular sushi fillings of tuna, salmon, and *hamachi* yellowtail are each paired with Spicy Mayonnaise Sauce. When served together, the black, green, and red colors pop on the plate.

BLACK SPICY ROLL (A)

GREEN SPICY ROLL (B)

RED SPICY ROLL (C)

MAKES 1 ROLL;
6 BITE-SIZED PIECES

½ cup (100 grams) sushi rice

½ sheet nori

1 strip sashimi-grade tuna (A) or salmon (B) or *hamachi* yellowtail (C), ½ inch (1 cm) thick, 8 inches (21 cm) long

1 to 2 stalks asparagus, blanched in salted water, cut into generous 8-inch (21-cm) lengths, and halved lengthwise if too thick

2 teaspoons Spicy Mayonnaise Sauce (PAGE 151)

toasted black sesame seeds (A) or finely chopped chives (B) or ground red chili powder (C)

soy sauce for dipping

Lay the nori crosswise on the plastic-covered *makisu,* shiny side down. Dampen both hands with ice-cold water and form the sushi rice into a log. Place it on the nori and spread out evenly, leaving a scant ½-inch (1-cm) strip uncovered at the upper edge but slightly extending beyond the nori at the lower edge. Scatter black sesame seeds (or chopped chives or chili powder) evenly over the rice. Pinch the nearest side of the nori with both fingers and flip over forward so that the nori is on top.

    Place the tuna (or salmon or *hamachi* yellowtail) strip and asparagus on the nori and add Spicy Mayonnaise Sauce. Roll and cut into 6 pieces. Serve with soy sauce. See instructions under California Roll (PAGE 31).

NEW YEAR'S LUCKY *FUTOMAKI* ROLL

For the Japanese, New Year is the most celebrated festival of the year. At NOBU we celebrate each year with this special extra-large (4-inch/10-cm diameter) *futomaki* roll that uses 3 sheets of nori, more than 1 pound (500 grams) of sushi rice, and 10 different fillings. Every December our Tokyo restaurant receives many takeout early orders for this roll.

MAKES 1 ROLL; 8 PIECES

2½ cups (500 grams) sushi rice

3 full sheets nori

1 Japanese cucumber, cut into 8-inch (21-cm) lengths, both ends removed

2 Boiled Japanese Tiger Prawns (PAGE 148)

meat of 3 boiled snow crab legs

⅔ ounce (20 grams) *komochi* kombu or *kazunoko* roe (PAGE 166) sliced and soaked in cold water overnight to reduce the salinity

1 strip Thick Baked Omelet (PAGE 149) or *Dashimaki* Omelet (PAGE 91) without sea urchin, ½ inch (1 cm) thick, 8 inches (21 cm) long

3 slices Vinegared Mackerel (PAGE 75)

3 slices Simmered *Anago* Eel (PAGE 150)

1 32-inch (80 cm/⅔ ounce/20 grams) ribbon Soy-Simmered *Kampyō* (PAGE 150)

2 to 3 Soy-Simmered Shiitaké Mushrooms (PAGE 148), squeezed of excess liquid and sliced

2 tablespoons chopped scallions

2 tablespoons *masago* roe

grated wasabi

BASIC TECHNIQUE FOR ROLLING A THICK ROLL:

1. Place one sheet of the nori shiny side down on the working surface. Smear a few grains of sushi rice on the upper edge. This will act as glue to join the second piece of nori to make one extra-long sheet. Form the sushi rice into a log with damp hands. Place it on upper side of the nori.

2. Spread the rice evenly up to the left and right edges without spilling over, leaving a 2-inch (5-cm) strip uncovered at the upper edge and a scant 2-inch (4-cm) strip at the lower edge. Place the third sheet of nori on the rice as shown.

3. Spread some wasabi across the nori. Place the cucumber across the end of the sushi rice close to you and arrange the rest of the fillings neatly, as shown. Make sure that some rice remains uncovered with fillings at the upper edge.

4. Pinch the lower edge of the nori with both fingers and start rolling, using the cucumber as the core of the roll.

5. Continue rolling to finish as tightly as possible. Try not to incorporate air between layers.

6. With damp fingers, gently press and neatly flatten the fillings at both ends of the roll. Cut into 8 pieces with a sharp knife, wiping the blade with a damp cloth after each cut.

OTHERS

DRAGON ROLL

The slices of avocado on the outside of this roll gives the appearance of a scaly dragon's back, hence Dragon Roll, which now can be found the world over. This also can be made using only vegetables.

MAKES 1 ROLL; 8 PIECES

Inside-Out Roll with Salmon and Asparagus (as core for Dragon Roll)

- ½ cup (100 grams) sushi rice
- ½ sheet nori
- 1 strip sashimi-grade salmon, ½ inch (1 cm) thick, 8 inches (21 cm) long
- 1 stalk asparagus, blanched in salted water, cut into generous 8-inch (21-cm) lengths, and halved lengthwise if too thick
- grated wasabi
- 1 to 2 teaspoons toasted white sesame seeds

1 avocado half, pit removed

1 teaspoon *masago* roe

soy sauce for dipping

Make an Inside-Out Roll with Salmon and Asparagus by following the procedure of California Roll (PAGE 31).

    Place the avocado half on a cutting board and slice diagonally as thin as possible, about 1/12 inch (2 mm) thick. Ideally the slices will be 3 inches (7.5 cm) long to cover the roll (PHOTO 1). Push the avocado slices at a right angle to the cut to let them fall over like dominos. Adjust until the same length as the roll. On the working surface, lay a piece of plastic wrap that is big enough to cover the avocado slices and the roll. Insert a large knife under the avocado slices and lift up (PHOTO 2). Turn the knife over to place the avocado on the plastic wrap, green side down. Spread *masago* roe on the avocado and set the inside-out roll on top (PHOTO 3). Lift up both edges of the plastic wrap, so that the avocado slices cover the roll. Turn the roll over (PHOTO 4). Cover the roll with the *makisu* and gently press the whole roll (PHOTO 5).

    Remove the *makisu* and plastic wrap (PHOTO 6). Cut the roll into 8 pieces with a sharp knife, wiping the blade with a damp cloth after each cut. Serve with soy sauce.

NOTE

The key point is to cut the avocado slices as thin as possible so that the slices can envelope the roll without breaking.

OTHERS

RAINBOW ROLL

The orange salmon, red tuna, white sea bream, and other fillings make up this iridescent Rainbow Roll, accentuated by *shiso* leaves for their green pop of color and flavor.

MAKES 1 ROLL; 6 PIECES

Inside-Out Roll with Snow Crab and Cucumber (as core for Rainbow Roll)

- ½ cup (100 grams) sushi rice
- ½ sheet nori
- meat of 2 boiled snow crab legs
- 2 thin cucumber sticks, generous 4 inches (10 cm) long
- grated wasabi
- 1 tablespoon toasted white sesame seeds

7 to 8 slices of sashimi-grade seafood such as tuna, salmon, sea bream (*tai*), Boiled Japanese Tiger Prawn (PAGE 148) or Vinegared *Kohada* (PAGE 76)

1 to 2 green *shiso* leaves

soy sauce for dipping

Make an Inside-Out Roll with Snow Crab and Cucumber, following the procedure of California Roll (PAGE 31).

Lay out the fish slices and green *shiso* leaves across the plastic wrap-covered *makisu* at about a 45° angle, as shown, partly overlapping each slice (PHOTO 1). Set the Inside-Out Roll on the fish slices (PHOTO 2). Cover the fish and roll with the *makisu* and shape the whole gently so that the toppings cover the roll. Cut the roll into 6 pieces with a sharp knife, wiping the blade with a damp cloth after each cut. Serve with soy sauce.

41

OTHERS

PICKLED *NOZAWANA* ROLL

Nozawana-zuké, a pickle of broad green leaves known for its pleasant tang, is used in lieu of nori for a subtle-flavored vegetable-wrapped roll. The sushi rice is balanced with the delicate condiments and sweet tomatoes.

MAKES 1 ROLL; 6 PIECES

⅔ cup (120 grams) sushi rice

1 to 2 leaves *nozawana-zuké* (pickled *nozawana* greens), store-bought

2-inch (5-cm) length Japanese leek (*naganégi*)

½ *myōga* bud, cut in half lengthwise

2 green *shiso* leaves, minced

1 teaspoon minced *gari* pickled ginger

1 teaspoon toasted white sesame seeds

2 to 4 cherry tomatoes cut into wedges

Score the Japanese leek lengthwise. Remove the light green core and discard. Julienne the leek, soak in cold water for a couple of minutes, drain, and blot dry. Thinly slice the *myōga* bud lengthwise, soak in cold water, drain, and blot dry.

   Mix the sushi rice, leek, *myōga*, *shiso* leaves, and *gari* pickled ginger in a bowl. Use cooking chopsticks to mix instead of a spatula or *shamoji* so that the rice doesn't get too sticky.

   Lay the *nozawana-zuké* leaves crosswise on the *makisu*, partly overlapping if 2 leaves are needed, to make an 8×5-inch (19×12-cm) sheet. Dampen both hands with ice-cold water, form the rice mixture into a log, and place it on the *nozawana* sheet. Spread the rice mixture evenly to the left and right edges without spilling over, leaving a 1-inch (2- to 3-cm) strip uncovered at the upper edge, and a scant 1-inch (2-cm) strip at the lower edge.

   Arrange the tomato wedges crosswise in the middle of the rice and roll. Cut into 6 pieces with a sharp knife, wiping the blade with a damp cloth after each cut.

PICKLED CHINESE CABBAGE ROLL

The salty and umami-rich pickled Chinese cabbage (*hakusai*) contrasts with the sweet crab legs and creamy avocado in this roll. The juicy and crisp texture of the cabbage gives the sensation of eating a salad.

MAKES 1 ROLL; 6 PIECES

⅔ cup (120 grams) sushi rice

1 to 2 leaves salt-pickled Chinese cabbage (*hakusai*), store-bought

meat of 4 boiled snow crab legs

2 thin cucumber sticks, generous 4 inches (10 cm) long

2 avocado wedges, cut lengthwise

Lay the pickled Chinese cabbage leaves crosswise on the *makisu*. Overlap two leaves, if needed, to make an 8×5-inch (19×12-cm) sheet. Dampen both hands with ice-cold water and form the sushi rice into a log and place it on the Chinese cabbage sheet. Spread the rice evenly to the left and right edges without spilling over, leaving a 1-inch (2- to 3-cm) strip uncovered at the upper edge and a scant 1-inch (2-cm) strip at the lower edge.

   Arrange the snow crab leg meat, cucumber, and avocado crosswise in the middle of the rice and roll. Cut into 6 pieces with a sharp knife, wiping the blade with a damp cloth after each cut.

CYLINDRICAL HAND ROLLS

CALIFORNIA HAND ROLL

The allure of eating hand rolls is to consume one as soon as it is rolled, while the nori is still crisp and is a dramatic contrast to the rich interior. Hand rolls are great fun for home parties, since the fillings are festive on the tabletop, and guests can enjoy the rolling experience.

MAKES 1 ROLL

¼ cup (50 grams) sushi rice
½ sheet nori
meat of 2 boiled snow crab legs
3 to 4 thin cucumber sticks, 4 inches (10 cm) long
1 avocado wedge, cut lengthwise
grated wasabi
soy sauce for dipping

BASIC TECHNIQUE FOR ROLLING A CYLINDRICAL HAND ROLL:
(Instructions are written for right-handed people. Reverse if you are left-handed.)

1 Hold the nori crosswise, shiny side down. Cut a small strip, about 1 inch (2.5 cm) wide, at the right edge of the nori, as shown in the photo. The top end of the piece should stay attached. Lay the nori on the fingers of your left hand and place the sushi rice on the side opposite the cut strip.

2 Dampen your right hand with ice-cold water and lightly spread the sushi rice on the nori.

3 Spread some wasabi and arrange the cucumber, snow crab, and avocado on the sushi rice.

4 With your right fingers, roll from the side close to you as tightly as possible, to make a cylinder. Just before finishing the rolling, tear off the strip and insert one end between the edge of the nori and the hand roll.

5 Wrap the bottom of the hand roll with the strip and hold it with your thumb, so that the rice and the fillings don't fall out when the roll is eaten. Serve with soy sauce.

NOTE

There are two methods for making hand rolls. The photos show the basic hand roll. This cylinder shape is easy to eat and offers the perfect balance of sushi rice to fillings with each bite.

The other technique for a hand roll is to make a cone. The presentation is very playful, and the rolls can be served in a glass as shown in the photo on PAGES **46-49**.

CONE-SHAPED HAND ROLLS

GRILLED KING CRAB HAND ROLL

Hot, grilled king crab leg meat is the backbone for this luxurious hand roll. It is accentuated with finely sliced vegetables, which contribute to its color, rich texture, and flavor.

MAKES 1 ROLL

¼ cup (50 grams) sushi rice

½ sheet nori

meat of 1 boiled king crab leg

salt and pepper

1 teaspoon olive oil

¼ cup finely julienned, 2-inch (5-cm) lengths of cucumber, daikon, carrot, and celery

grated wasabi

soy sauce for dipping

Lay the boiled king crab leg meat on a cooking tray, season with salt and pepper, and drizzle with olive oil. Grill on the *yakiami* grill until browned or cook in a toaster oven for about 5 minutes.

Crisp julienned vegetables in cold water for a couple of minutes, drain, and blot dry. Mix well.

Lay the nori crosswise on the fingers of your left hand, shiny side down. Use the first two steps of the California Hand Roll (PAGE 45), but no strip-cutting is needed. Spread some wasabi on the rice. Top with the vegetable mixture and king crab meat.

With your right fingers, roll as tightly as possible from the side close to you to make a cone. Serve with soy sauce.

CONE-SHAPED HAND ROLLS

LEMON HAND ROLL

Lemon, cucumbers, and green *shiso* leaves make up this roll, which is very light on the palate. Make sure to use thinly sliced cucumbers, which go well with the lemon's delicate flavor and the *shiso* leaves' refreshing aroma. The Lemon Hand Roll is a great palate cleanser and often recommended to diners at NOBU restaurants.

MAKES 1 ROLL

¼ cup (50 grams) sushi rice

½ sheet nori

1 green *shiso* leaf

4 to 5 thin cucumber sticks, 4 inches (10 cm) long

¼ lemon *supreme*, flesh only, no peel

grated wasabi

½ teaspoon toasted white sesame seeds

Shōyu-Jio (PAGE 169)

Lay the nori crosswise on the fingers of your left hand, shiny side down. Use the first two steps of the California Hand Roll (PAGE 45), but no strip-cutting is needed. Spread some wasabi and arrange the *shiso* leaf, cucumber, and lemon *supreme* on the rice. Scatter toasted sesame seeds and top with *Shōyu-Jio*.

    With your right fingers, roll as tightly as possible from the side close to you, to make a cone.

47

COLORFUL SOY SHEET HAND ROLLS

Soy sheets, also called soy paper wraps, are popular in the West. Made from soybeans and used in lieu of nori, these healthful, colorful sheets are perfect for finger food at a party.

CONE-SHAPED HAND ROLLS

MAKES 1 ROLL EACH

YELLOW

¼ cup (50 grams) sushi rice

½ yellow soy sheet (full sheet cut in half lengthwise)

meat of 1 boiled snow crab leg

1 thin avocado slice

1 thin cucumber stick, 4 inches (10 cm) long

grated wasabi

soy sauce for dipping

PINK

¼ cup (50 grams) sushi rice

½ pink soy sheet (full sheet cut in half lengthwise)

1 to 2 green *shiso* leaves

1 pickled burdock root, store-bought

1 thin avocado slice

1 okra pod, stemmed and sepals removed

1 thin cucumber stick, 4 inches (10 cm) long

kaiwaré daikon sprouts

grated wasabi

soy sauce for dipping

GREEN

¼ cup (50 grams) sushi rice

½ green soy sheet (full sheet cut in half lengthwise)

1 thin cucumber stick, 4 inches (10 cm) long

1 strip Simmered *Anago* Eel (PAGE 150), (roughly the same size as the cucumber)

grated wasabi

soy sauce for dipping

SESAME SEED

¼ cup (50 grams) sushi rice

½ sesame soy sheet (full sheet cut in half lengthwise)

Rock Shrimp Tempura

2 fresh rock shrimp, deveined, heads, tails, shells removed

½ beaten egg, chilled

scant ½ cup (100 ml) ice-cold water

½ cup (50 grams) cake flour or all-purpose flour

oil for deep-frying

Spicy Mayonnaise Sauce (PAGE 151)

yuzu juice

soy sauce for dipping

Rock Shrimp Tempura: Mix the egg and ice-cold water in a bowl. Add ½ cup (50 grams) flour and mix lightly. Dip rock shrimp in the batter and deep-fry in oil at 340°F (170°C) until crisp (See Shrimp Tempura Roll, PAGE 32). Toss the shrimp with a small amount of Spicy Mayonnaise Sauce and *yuzu* juice to taste in a bowl.

Instructions for Four Rolls: Lay the soy sheet crosswise on the fingers of your left hand. Use the first two steps of the California Hand Roll (PAGE 45), but no strip-cutting is needed. Spread some wasabi if needed. Arrange the fillings of each roll on the sushi rice.

With your right fingers, roll as tightly as possible into a cone from the side close to you. Serve with soy sauce.

NOTE

Soy sheets are edible sheets made from soybean protein and other flavorings such as sesame, turmeric, spinach, and paprika. Soy sheets are sold at Asian supermarkets.

49

NOBU HAND ROLL SUSHI PARTY BOX

ASSORTED FILLINGS FOR HAND ROLLS

SUSHI RICE AND BAMBOO SPATULA

SAUCES, PICKLES, WASABI, NORI, SOY SAUCE, AND OTHER CONDIMENTS

Hand rolls are often served at home parties in Japan to welcome friends and family when they gather for an occasion. Guests can select their own fillings, create combinations as they like, and roll the sushi on their own for an entertaining and memorable meal.

Sushi has long been popular outside of Japan as a healthful and delicious party food. NOBU New York will deliver sushi rolls to your home, or for freshly made hand rolls, the NOBU Hand Roll Sushi Party Box can be ordered. At the appointed time, a staff member from NOBU New York will deliver an impressive three-tiered box of paulownia wood imprinted with the NOBU name. The three tiers contain an assortment of fillings, sushi rice, and all of the necessary condiments. The fillings are deftly and attractively arranged to reflect Japanese and Nobu's aesthetic sense.

One tier includes the indispensable fillings of tuna, salmon, and *hamachi* yellowtail. Snow crab legs, cucumber, and avocado are included for California Rolls, as well as boiled prawns, sea bream, and omelet, to name but a few. The colorful and luscious fillings are sure to make an impression for any occasion. In another tier, sushi rice is divided into single-serving portion sizes, and a bamboo spatula is included to serve it. The third tier includes pre-cut nori, spicy mayonnaise to make spicy rolls, a mellow avocado mayonnaise, as well as sesame seeds, *masago* roe, wasabi, soy sauce, and other popular condiments for hand rolls.

After the guest places his/her order, the host may make the hand roll or guide the guest in the pleasant art of rolling one's own. Rolls can be placed in a glass for a dramatic presentation or eaten right away for the best flavor. Hand roll sushi parties are a luxurious and fun way to entertain at home.

Nigiri sushi originated in Edo (now Tokyo) during the Edo period (1603–1868). A portion of rice is topped with fresh seafood or another topping and gently formed into a bite-sized morsel. Here Nobu teaches you the basic techniques to make authentic nigiri sushi, and he also shares many recipes for the beautiful, delicious, and original NOBU Style sushi that can be found at his restaurants.

Nigiri-Zushi

NIG

IRI SUSHI

NIGIRI SUSHI

BASIC NIGIRI HAND-FORMING TECHNIQUE

(All instructions in this chapter are written for right-handed people. Reverse if you are left-handed.)

The secret to making good nigiri sushi is not to squeeze too hard when forming. There should be just enough pressure so that the sushi rice sticks together while leaving enough air to keep it light. When eaten, it should immediately fall apart, and the flavor of the sushi rice should blossom in your mouth.

Here I introduce the eleven basic steps in detail for making nigiri sushi. Since the toppings are mostly made from raw seafood, it is essential to work as quickly as possible so as not to spoil the seafood with the heat generated from your hands. Of course, at first it may take a while, but with practice you will develop a rhythm, and the process will become natural.

Steps 5, 8, and 11 are perhaps the hardest to master. The left hand keeps the rice in shape, and index and middle fingers of the right hand gently press down on the rice or on the topping on the rice. The left hand should just hold the shape of the sushi rice, and the right hand will cover the rice or topping and just bring it together.

1 Prepare sashimi-grade fish slices for nigiri sushi (see PAGE 14). Lay one piece on the fingers of your left hand.

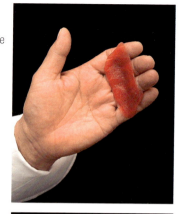

2 Pick up some grated wasabi with the index finger of your right hand and spread it on the fish.

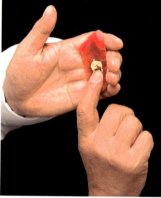

3 Moisten your right hand with ice-cold water. Pick up generous 1 tablespoon (½ ounce/15 grams) of sushi rice for one piece of nigiri sushi. With your right hand, shape a loose form of rice and set it on the fish slice.

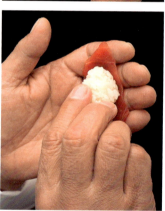

4 With your left thumb, lightly press the middle of the rice form to loosen and incorporate some air. With your right thumb and index fingers squeeze the rice very lightly to prevent any from spilling.

NIGIRI SUSHI

5 Curve your left palm and place your right index and middle fingers over the top of the rice and shape very gently.

9 Turn the sushi 180 degrees with your right hand.

6 With your left thumb, roll the sushi towards the tips of your fingers so that the fish is on top.

10 Repeat step 7.

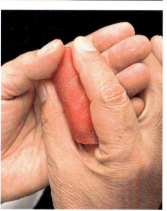

7 Make both long sides of the sushi straight. Shape with your right thumb and index finger by gliding from the top of the fish down to the long sides of the rice.

11 Repeat step 8.

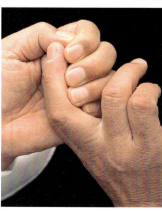

8 Curve your left palm and place your right index and middle fingers over the top of the fish and shape very gently.

12 Set the nigiri sushi on a serving plate. Serve with soy sauce.

57

NIGIRI SUSHI

SALT-CURED TUNA NIGIRI

Curing seafood in salt is a technique that is often used in Japan. In this recipe, tuna in the shape of a *saku* block (PAGE 14) is covered with a generous amount of salt and set aside. This process removes some water from the fish while increasing the umami, and it also changes the texture. The color of the tuna may surprise you, since the shades of red change in the curing process. The texture and flavor of salt-cured tuna becomes richer.

MAKES 2 PIECES

generous 2 tablespoons (30 grams) sushi rice

Salt-Cured Tuna

> 1 *saku* block (PAGE 14) of sashimi-grade tuna
> the same amount of salt as tuna by weight

grated wasabi

soy sauce for dipping

Salt-Cured Tuna: Spread the salt in a cooking tray and place the tuna *saku* on the salt. Fully coat the tuna generously with salt. Transfer onto a flat sieve or a wire rack with another cooking tray underneath to catch drippings from the fish. Cover with plastic wrap and refrigerate for 40 minutes.

Rinse the salt off the tuna and blot dry. Cut 2 slices from one end of the Salt-Cured Tuna *saku* (PAGE 14).

To make nigiri: Place one tuna slice on the fingers of your left hand. Spread some wasabi on the tuna, top with half of the sushi rice, and shape into nigiri sushi. Repeat with the second slice. Serve with soy sauce.

Salt-Cured Tuna will keep for up to 3 days tightly wrapped in plastic wrap and refrigerated.

NIGIRI SUSHI

SEARED TUNA NIGIRI

Sliced fatty tuna is scored in a crosshatch pattern and lightly seared on one side. The fat melts, sinews become tender, and searing brings a toasty aroma to the fish. This is best when served with Garlic Soy Sauce. The contrast in flavor and texture of the two different sides is what makes this dish unique.

MAKES 2 PIECES

generous 2 tablespoons (30 grams) sushi rice
2 slices sashimi-grade medium-fatty tuna (*chūtoro*)
Garlic Soy Sauce (PAGE 151)
grated wasabi

Finely score one side of the tuna slices in a crosshatch pattern. If the flesh is fibrous, score the side with more fibers, because the sinews become tender and tastier when broiled.

Preheat a *yakiami* grill over medium-high heat. Sear only the scored side of the tuna slices for about 20 seconds. Put the seared tuna in Garlic Soy Sauce and marinate for 1 to 2 minutes.

Place one tuna slice on the fingers of your left hand, cooked side facing up. Spread some wasabi on the fish, top with half of the sushi rice, and shape into nigiri sushi. Repeat with the second slice.

NIGIRI SUSHI

FLOUNDER *TIRADITO* NIGIRI

Tiradito with *Shōyu-Jio* is one of NOBU's signature nigiri sushi. The spicy *rocoto* chili pepper paste, acidic lemon and *yuzu* juice, and salty *Shōyu-Jio* compliment the delicate white fish and come together for a perfect bite.

MAKES 2 PIECES

generous 2 tablespoons (30 grams) sushi rice

2 slices sashimi-grade flounder

2 coriander leaves

chili paste, preferably made from *rocoto* chili

Shōyu-Jio (PAGE 169)

½ teaspoon *yuzu* juice

1 teaspoon lemon juice

Place one flounder slice on the fingers of your left hand. Top with half of the sushi rice and shape into nigiri sushi. Repeat with the second slice.

Arrange both pieces of nigiri sushi on a serving plate. Garnish each sushi with a coriander leaf, chili paste, and *Shōyu-Jio*. In a small bowl combine *yuzu* and lemon juice and drizzle over the pieces.

NOBU-STYLE 3

TIRADITO

"*Tirar*" in Spanish means "to throw." In Peru the origins of this dish comes from throwing fresh seafood into a bowl with citrus juice and fresh chili peppers and mixing it all together. Similar to ceviche, this dish was most likely influenced by Japanese immigrants who introduced sashimi to the culture. This *tiradito* recipe created by Nobu is garnished with green coriander leaves and dotted with red *rocoto* paste, made from a very hot South American chili pepper, and then sprinkled with a citrus juice. This simple technique and presentation based on a traditional *tiradito* is a classic NOBU-Style dish.

NIGIRI SUSHI

KATSUOBUSHI AND KOMBU-CURED FLOUNDER NIGIRI

Kobu-jimé (kombu-*jimé*) is a clasic Japanese technique. Two sheets of kombu kelp are used to sandwich raw seafood or vegetables. To make this dish even more delicious, *katsuobushi* is added, since it is rich in inosinic acid, while kombu is touted for its glutamates. When those two are combined, the synergistic effect brings on an even richer umami, which has been proven in scientific studies.

MAKES 2 PIECES

generous 2 tablespoons (30 grams) sushi rice

Katsuobushi and Kombu-Cured Flounder

1 fillet sashimi-grade flounder, skin removed

2 kombu sheets, larger than the flounder fillet, preferably Rausu kombu

saké

salt

½ to 1 ounce (20 grams) *katsuobushi* flakes

grated wasabi

soy sauce for dipping

Katsuobushi and Kombu-Cured Flounder: Dampen a small piece of paper towel with saké and lightly wipe the kombu sheets to soften them. Lightly sprinkle salt on the both sides of the fillet and fully cover with *katsuobushi* flakes. Lay one softened kombu sheet in a large cooking tray. Set the *katsuobushi*-covered fillet on the kombu and cover with the second kombu sheet. Tightly cover with plastic wrap and refrigerate for 5 to 6 hours.

To make nigiri: Remove the flounder fillet from the kombu sheets and cut off 2 slices (PAGE 14). Place one flounder slice on the fingers of your left hand. Spread some wasabi on the flounder, top with half of the sushi rice, and shape into nigiri sushi. Repeat with the second slice. Serve with soy sauce.

The *Katsuobushi* and Kombu-Cured Flounder will keep for up to 3 days if removed from kombu, tightly wrapped in plastic wrap, and refrigerated.

NOTE

- If using several small pieces of kombu for curing, make sure they fully cover the flounder fillet.
- Kombu sheets can be reused for curing fish 4 to 5 times if wiped with a saké-dampened cloth and dried thoroughly after every use. Once the kombu has been used for curing fish, it should never be reused for curing vegetables (PAGES 100, 124).

NIGIRI SUSHI

DRIED MULLET ROE OVER SEA BREAM NIGIRI

Karasumi, dried mullet roe, is a luxury preserved food that is widely enjoyed in Japan. Light grilling releases some of its aromas and brings out its umami. The mullet roe is powdered on a grater and sprinkled over sea bream sashimi for a beautiful and delicious sushi. Green *shiso* leaf is layered between the sushi rice and sea bream to bring a cool sensation. It goes without saying that *karasumi* and saké is a match made in heaven.

MAKES 2 PIECES

generous 2 tablespoons (30 grams) sushi rice
1 lobe *karasumi* (dried mullet roe)
2 slices sashimi-grade sea bream (*tai*)
1 green *shiso* leaf, cut in half
grated wasabi
soy sauce for dipping

Cover the *karasumi* with aluminum foil. Heat in a toaster oven or in a frying pan over low heat for 20 minutes. When the *karasumi* is heated through, it becomes even harder. Let cool, peel, and discard the translucent skin. Grate the *karasumi* to a powder with a fine grater.

　Place one sea bream slice on the fingers of your left hand and spread some wasabi. Layer with half a green *shiso* leaf, top with half of the sushi rice, and shape into nigiri sushi. Repeat with the second slice. Sprinkle 1 tablespoon of *karasumi* powder over the sea bream. Serve with soy sauce.

　The *karasumi* powder will keep for up to 1 month refrigerated in an airtight container.

NIGIRI SUSHI

YELLOWTAIL AND JALAPEÑO NIGIRI

A slice of jalapeño chili and grated garlic contrast the rich *hamachi* yellowtail. Jalapeño's piquancy is quite different from wasabi and makes an interesting addition to the nigiri palette. Yuzu Soy Sauce brings a nice acidity and aroma that lightens the fatty fish.

MAKES 2 PIECES

generous 2 tablespoons (30 grams) sushi rice
2 slices sashimi-grade *hamachi* yellowtail
¼ teaspoon grated garlic
2 thin slices of jalapeño chili
Yuzu Soy Sauce (PAGE 151)

Place one *hamachi* yellowtail slice on the fingers of your left hand. Top with half of the sushi rice and shape into nigiri sushi. Repeat with the second slice.

Arrange both pieces of nigiri sushi on a serving plate. Garnish with grated garlic and jalapeño chili. Serve with Yuzu Soy Sauce.

FLASH-SEARED YELLOWTAIL NIGIRI

Buri, a mature yellowtail, is touted for its rich, buttery fat. *Buri* is flash-seared to melt the fat and to bring out its delicious aromas. To balance the dish, it is served with grated daikon and *kinomé*, the aromatic young leaves of the *sanshō* bush.

MAKES 2 PIECES

generous 2 tablespoons (30 grams) sushi rice

2 slices sashimi-grade *buri* yellowtail

grated wasabi

2-inch (5-cm) daikon segment

1 teaspoon Yuzu Soy Sauce (PAGE 151)

2 sprigs *kinomé*

Peel and grate the daikon and drain. Lightly squeeze out and discard most of the liquid from the grated daikon. Transfer the daikon to a bowl. Add Yuzu Soy Sauce and mix.

Make several shallow scores lengthwise on one side of the *buri* yellowtail slices. Preheat a *yakiami* grill over medium-high heat. Sear only the scored side of the *buri* slices for about 3 to 5 seconds.

Place one *buri* slice on the fingers of your left hand, seared side facing down. Spread some wasabi on the *buri*, top with half of the sushi rice, and shape into nigiri sushi. Repeat with the second slice.

Arrange both pieces of nigiri sushi on a serving plate. Garnish with the Yuzu Soy Sauce and grated daikon mixture and top with *kinomé*.

NIGIRI SUSHI

SALMON NEW STYLE SASHIMI NIGIRI

New Style Sashimi is one of NOBU's basic signature techniques (PAGE 27). Salmon is lightly cooked, giving it a different flavor profile from raw salmon.

MAKES 2 PIECES

generous 2 tablespoons (30 grams) sushi rice

2 slices sashimi-grade salmon

1 small knob ginger, peeled and very finely julienned (*hari shōga*; see PAGE 26)

2 to 3 chives, cut into the same size as ginger

⅛ teaspoon finely grated garlic

¼ teaspoon toasted white sesame seeds

1 teaspoon Yuzu Soy Sauce (PAGE 151)

New Style Oil (PAGE 151)

grated wasabi

Soak the julienned ginger in a bowl of cold water for 2 to 3 minutes. Drain and blot dry with a paper towel.

    Lay salmon slices on a plate or small cooking tray, and lightly spread grated garlic on the salmon. Arrange with ginger and chives, and sprinkle with sesame seeds. Drizzle Yuzu Soy Sauce. Put a small amount of New Style Oil in a saucepan and heat until it just starts to smoke. Drizzle 1 teaspoon of the heated oil over the salmon. Cover with a paper towel and lightly press to blot any excess liquid.

    Divide the sushi rice into 2 parts and make 2 rice nigiri forms. Spread some wasabi on one of the rice nigiri forms, top with the salmon slice, and shape into nigiri sushi. Be careful when shaping it, since the cooked salmon is flakey. Repeat with the second nigiri rice form.

LEMON-CURED SALMON NIGIRI

Curing salmon in lemon helps to balance the rich fat. However, if the fish absorbs too much acidity, the umami will be difficult to sense, so it should be cured for only a short time. A garnish of julienned truffles provides a unique texture and rich aroma.

MAKES 2 PIECES

generous 2 tablespoons (30 grams) sushi rice

Lemon-Cured Salmon
- 1 *saku* block (PAGE 14) of sashimi-grade salmon
- a 50/50 mixture of salt and sugar that weighs the same as the salmon
- freshly squeezed lemon juice, 1 cup (250 ml) or enough to cover the fish

grated wasabi

julienned black truffles

2 baby green *shiso* leaves

soy sauce for dipping

Lemon-Cured Salmon: Combine the salt and granulated sugar and spread on a cooking tray. Lay the salmon *saku* in the tray and fully coat with a generous amount of the salt and sugar mixture. Transfer onto a flat sieve or a wire rack with another cooking tray underneath to catch any drippings from the fish. Wrap the salmon and tray with plastic wrap and refrigerate for 3 hours. Rinse off the salt-sugar mixture and blot dry with a paper towel. Place the salmon in an acid-resistant container and add the lemon juice until it just covers the fish. Cover and cure in a refrigerator for 30 minutes. Do not cure any longer, or the salmon will become sour. Discard the lemon juice. Blot the salmon dry with a paper towel.

To make nigiri: Cut off 2 slices from the Lemon-Cured Salmon *saku* (page 14). Place one salmon slice on the fingers of your left hand. Spread some wasabi on the salmon, top with half of the sushi rice, and shape into nigiri sushi. Repeat with the second slice. Arrange both pieces of nigiri sushi on a serving plate. Garnish with black truffles and *shiso* leaves. Serve with soy sauce.

The Lemon-Cured Salmon will keep for up to 3 days tightly wrapped in plastic wrap and refrigerated.

VINEGARED MACKEREL NIGIRI

HIKARIMONO

Silver-and-blue-skinned fish like mackerel, *aji*, and *kohada* are collectively called *hikarimono* ("things that shine"). Fish in this group have long been appreciated in Japan for their characteristic flavor. Most of the fish in this category tend to spoil quickly, and before refrigeration, the traditional method of preserving these fish was to cure them in vinegar. It is still popular today to enjoy these shining fish lightly cured in vinegar.

To make vinegar-cured *hikarimono*, first, filet or butterfly the fish and cover in a specified amount of salt to rid it of excess water. This step also helps to eliminate some of the odor typical of this type of seafood. As excess water is removed, the flesh becomes firm, which helps to prevent it from falling apart when it's later cured in vinegar. For more specific instructions, see the recipes on the following pages. Please keep in mind that fattier fish will need more salt and time to cure.

MAKES 2 PIECES

generous 2 tablespoons (30 grams) sushi rice

Vinegared Mackerel

| 2 sashimi-grade mackerel fillets (PAGE 153)
| salt
| rice vinegar or grain vinegar

grated ginger
chopped scallions or chives
soy sauce for dipping

1

2

Vinegared Mackerel: Spread a generous amount of salt in a cooking tray. Lay the mackerel fillets on the salt and fully coat with the salt (PHOTO 1). Transfer onto a flat sieve or a wire rack with another cooking tray underneath to catch any drippings from the fish (PHOTO 2). Cover with plastic wrap and refrigerate for 1 to 2 hours (longer for bigger or fattier fillets). Rinse the salt off the mackerel and blot dry.

Place the fillets in an acid-resistant container and add vinegar until it just covers the fillets (PHOTO 3). Cover and refrigerate for 30 minutes, turning the fillets once after 15 minutes.

Rinse off the salt and blot dry (PHOTO 4). Cut away the rib bones with a knife and remove the pin bones with tweezers.

The Vinegared Mackerel (and all the other vinegared fish shown on PAGES 75 and 76) will keep for up to 3 days tightly covered in plastic wrap and refrigerated.

To make nigiri: Gently peel off the thin and translucent skin of the Vinegared Mackerel fillets. Start from the head end and carefully peel towards the tail, leaving the blackish-silvery inner skin attached to the flesh. Cut off 2 slices from one end of the fillet (PAGE 14).

Place one mackerel slice on the fingers of your left hand. Lay half of the sushi rice on the slice and shape it into nigiri sushi. Repeat with the second slice. Garnish both nigiri pieces with a small amount of grated ginger and chopped scallions or chives. Serve with soy sauce.

3

4

NOTE

Preserving the shining colors of the fish is most important in this process. To best preserve the color, when soaking in vinegar, a general rule is to place the fish flesh side down into the vinegar. (In the case of larger fish like mackerel, the filet will be turned over during the course of curing in vinegar.) Blue and silver shades appear between the thin skin and the flesh of the fish. To showcase these gorgeous colors, the skin is gently peeled off when making nigiri sushi

NIGIRI SUSHI

VINEGARED *AJI* NIGIRI

MAKES 2 PIECES

generous 2 tablespoons (30 grams) sushi rice

Vinegared *Aji*
- 1 sashimi-grade *aji* (horse mackerel; 6 inches/15 cm), butterflied (PAGE 154)
- salt
- rice vinegar or grain vinegar

grated ginger

soy sauce for dipping

Vinegared *Aji*: Lay the *aji* on a flat sieve or a wire rack with a cooking tray underneath. Evenly sprinkle a little salt on both sides of the fish (PHOTO). Cover with plastic wrap and refrigerate for 10 minutes. Rinse the salt off the fish and blot dry.

Place the *aji* in an acid-resistant container, flesh side down. Add vinegar until it just covers the fish. Cover and refrigerate for 8 minutes. Drain and blot dry.

To make nigiri: Gently peel away the thin and translucent skin of the Vinegared *Aji* (see Vinegared Mackerel). Cut the fish lengthwise to make 2 fillets, cut off the tail, and trim the edges. Make one deep score down the length of both pieces.

Place one *aji* piece on the fingers of your left hand, skin side down. Put grated ginger on the *aji*, then half of the sushi rice, and shape into nigiri sushi. Repeat with the second piece. Serve with soy sauce.

VINEGARED SARDINE NIGIRI

MAKES 2 PIECES

generous 2 tablespoons (30 grams) sushi rice

Vinegared Sardine
- 1 sashimi-grade sardine (*iwashi*; 6 to 7 inches/16 to 17 cm long), butterflied (PAGE 157)
- salt
- rice vinegar or grain vinegar

grated wasabi

soy sauce for dipping

Vinegared Sardine: Lay the sardine on a flat sieve or a wire rack with a cooking tray underneath. Evenly sprinkle a little salt on both sides of the fish. Cover with plastic wrap and refrigerate for 10 to 13 minutes. Rinse the salt off the fish and blot dry.

Place the sardine in an acid-resistant container, flesh side down. Add vinegar until it just covers the fish. Cover and refrigerate for 8 minutes. Drain and blot dry.

To make nigiri: Gently peel away the thin and translucent skin of the Vinegared Sardine (see Vinegared Mackerel). Cut the fish lengthwise to make 2 fillets, cut off the tail, and trim the edges.

Place one sardine piece on the fingers of your left hand, skin side down. Spread some wasabi on the sardine, top with half of the sushi rice, and shape into nigiri sushi. Repeat with the second piece. Serve with soy sauce.

VINEGARED *KOHADA* NIGIRI

MAKES 2 PIECES

generous 2 tablespoons (30 grams) sushi rice

Vinegared *Kohada*
- 1 sashimi-grade *kohada* (gizzard shad; 6 to 7 inches/16 to 17 cm long), butterflied (same way as *sayori*, PAGE 155)
- salt
- rice vinegar or grain vinegar

grated wasabi

soy sauce for dipping

Vinegared *Kohada*: Spread a generous amount of salt in a cooking tray. Lay the butterflied *kohada* on the salt and fully coat with the salt. Transfer onto a flat sieve or a wire rack with another cooking tray underneath. Cover with plastic wrap and refrigerate for 10 to 15 minutes. Rinse the salt off the fish and blot dry.

Place the *kohada* in an acid-resistant container, flesh side down. Add vinegar until it just covers the fish. Cover and refrigerate for 6 to 10 minutes. Drain and blot dry.

To make nigiri: Cut the Vinegared *Kohada* lengthwise to make 2 fillets. Cut off the tail and trim the edges. Cut in half lengthwise and overlap one piece on the other. Place one set of fish on the fingers of your left hand, skin side down. Spread some wasabi on the *kohada*, top with half of the sushi rice, and shape into nigiri sushi. Repeat with the second set. Serve with soy sauce.

NIGIRI SUSHI

VINEGARED *MAMÉ AJI* NIGIRI

MAKES 2 PIECES

generous 2 tablespoons (30 grams) sushi rice

Vinegared *Mamé Aji*
- 2 sashimi-grade *mamé aji* (baby horse mackerel; 3 to 4 inches/ 8 to 10 cm long), butterflied with head attached (PAGE 156)
- salt
- rice vinegar or grain vinegar

grated ginger

soy sauce for dipping

Vinegared *Mamé Aji*: Lay the *mamé aji* on a flat or regular sieve with a cooking tray underneath. Evenly sprinkle a little salt on both sides of the fish. Cover with plastic wrap and refrigerate for 10 minutes. Rinse the salt off the fish and blot dry.

Prepare an acid-resistant container filled with vinegar and place a small bowl upside down in it. Lay the *mamé aji* on the bowl, allowing only the head to be submerged in the vinegar (PHOTO). Cover with plastic wrap and refrigerate for 25 minutes. Remove the bowl and soak the whole fish in vinegar for another 5 minutes. (The head should be marinated longer than the rest of the fish, allowing the head to become soft enough to eat.) Drain and blot dry.

To make nigiri: Place one Vinegared *Mamé Aji* on the fingers of your left hand, skin side down. Put the grated ginger on the *mamé aji*, top with half of the sushi rice, and shape into nigiri sushi. Repeat with the second fish. Serve with soy sauce.

VINEGARED *SANMA* NIGIRI

MAKES 2 PIECES

generous 2 tablespoons (30 grams) sushi rice

Vinegared *Sanma*
- 1 sashimi-grade *sanma* (Pacific saury), butterflied (same way as *sayori*, PAGE 155)
- rice vinegar or grain vinegar
- salt

***Sanma* Liver Paste**
- 1 sashimi-grade *sanma* liver
- soy sauce

grated wasabi

Vinegared *Sanma*: Lay the *sanma* on a flat sieve or a wire rack with a cooking tray underneath. Evenly sprinkle a little salt on both sides of the fish. Cover with plastic wrap and refrigerate for 20 minutes. Rinse the salt off the fish and blot dry.

Place the *sanma* in an acid-resistant container, flesh side down. Add vinegar until it just covers the fish. Cover and refrigerate for 10 minutes. Drain and blot dry.

Sanma Liver Paste: Wrap the *sanma* liver in aluminum foil. Heat on a frying pan over low heat for about 5 minutes until the liver is cooked through. Remove the foil. Press the heated liver through a fine sieve with a spatula to make into paste. Mix soy sauce into the liver paste drop by drop until it is a thick liquid.

To make nigiri: Gently peel away the thin and translucent skin of the Vinegared *Sanma* (see Vinegered Mackerel). Cut the fish lengthwise to make 2 fillets, cut off the tail, and trim the edges. Cut off 2 pieces (3 inches/7.5 cm long) from one fillet, and make several scores lengthwise on the skin side of both pieces. Place one *sanma* piece on the fingers of your left hand, skin side down. Spread some wasabi, top with half of the sushi rice, and shape into nigiri sushi. Repeat with the second piece. Garnish with a little *Sanma* Liver Paste and serve.

SAYORI NIGIRI

MAKES 2 PIECES

generous 2 tablespoons (30 grams) sushi rice

1 sashimi-grade *sayori* (halfbeak; 12 to 16 inches/30 cm to 40 cm long), butterflied and head removed (PAGE 155)

grated wasabi

2 sprigs *kinomé*

soy sauce for dipping

Cut the butterflied *sayori* lengthwise to make 2 fillets. Place 1 fillet on the cutting board, skin side down, with the head end on the left. Gently insert a knife at the head end of a fillet between the skin and the flesh. Holding the head end of the skin firmly in place with your left hand, move the blade towards the tail end with a sawing motion to remove the skin (PHOTO 1). Try to leave the silvery inner skin intact. Trim the edges. Repeat with the second fillet.

To make nigiri: Turn and twist the tail and put under the left side of the fillet (PHOTO 2). Place one piece on the fingers of your left hand, skin side down. Spread some wasabi on the fish, top with half of the sushi rice, and shape into nigiri sushi. Repeat with the second piece. Garnish both nigiri pieces with *kinomé* and serve with soy sauce.

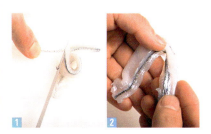

77

NIGIRI SUSHI

KOMBU-CURED *KISU* NIGIRI

MAKES 2 PIECES

generous 2 tablespoons (30 grams) sushi rice

Kombu-Cured *Kisu*

- 1 sashimi-grade *kisu* (sillago; 7 to 8 inches/18 cm to 20 cm long), butterflied (same way as *sayori*, PAGE 155)
- salt
- 2 kombu sheets, preferably Rausu kombu, but other varieties will also work
- saké

Shrimp Crumbles

- 3⅓ ounces (100 grams) small- to medium-sized fresh shrimp, heads and shells removed
- 1 tablespoon + 1 teaspoon (20 ml) saké
- 1 tablespoon + 1 teaspoon (20 ml) mirin
- ½ cup (100g) granulated sugar

grated wasabi

soy sauce for dipping

Kombu-Cured *Kisu*: Evenly sprinkle both sides of the *kisu* with a little salt. Lay the *kisu* on a flat sieve or a wire rack, skin side up, and place in a clean sink. Pour boiling water over the fish until the skin shrinks a little and the flesh becomes translucent (PHOTO 1). This makes the skin tender and edible. Immediately transfer the *kisu* to ice-cold water to cool. Drain and blot dry.

Dampen a small piece of paper towel with saké and lightly wipe the kombu sheets to soften them. Lay one kombu sheet on a cooking tray, set the fish on the kombu and cover with the second kombu sheet. Tightly cover with plastic wrap and refrigerate for 30 minutes to 1 hour.

Shrimp Crumbles (yields about 3 cups, of which ⅔ cup is used for this dish): Gently boil the shrimp in hot water until firm to touch. Place in a food processor and puree.

Place the shrimp puree in a saucepan over very low heat. Holding 3 to 5 chopsticks in one hand, break up the shrimp puree into fine crumbles and stir until the puree is dry (PHOTO 2). The crumbles may stick to the pan while drying, which is normal. Be sure to keep the heat low enough so the crumbles do not burn.

Add saké, mirin, and sugar to season in this order, while continuously stirring to prevent it from burning. After the liquid has dissipated and the crumbles become dry, remove from heat and sift through a large mesh sieve. Put any shrimp crumbles left on the sieve back into the saucepan and continue to break up the lumps and dry over very low heat. Sift through the sieve again. Repeat until completed.

Shrimp Crumbles will keep for up to 3 days refrigerated in a clean container.

To make nigiri: Cut the Kombu-Cured *Kisu* lengthwise to make 2 fillets. Cut off the tail and trim the edges. Make one deep score lengthwise on both pieces.

Place one *kisu* piece on the fingers of your left hand, skin side down. Spread some wasabi on the *kisu*, add some Shrimp Crumbles and half of the sushi rice, and shape into nigiri sushi. Repeat with the second piece. Serve with soy sauce.

NIGIRI SUSHI

SQUID "NOODLE" NIGIRI

Squid is cut into thin "noodles," and enough for one serving is placed over the sushi rice and gently pressed into nigiri sushi. There is a special cutting technique to best appreciate the soft texture and sweetness of the squid.

MAKES 2 PIECES

generous 2 tablespoons (30 grams) sushi rice

1 sashimi-grade squid body, cleaned and butterflied (PAGE 159)

grated wasabi

Dry Miso (PAGE 168)

Place the butterflied squid body sideways and cut off a 3-inch (7-cm) strip (PHOTO 1). To make very thin "noodles," the squid first needs to be sliced laterally into two very thin sheets. Hold the blade of the knife parallel to the cutting board surface and slice back and forth with your right hand while pushing down on the squid with your left hand (PHOTO 2). Finely julienne (⅛ inch/2 to 3 mm) the squid as shown.

Pick up just enough strands to cover the nigiri of julienned squid and hold with the fingers of your left hand. Spread some wasabi on the squid, top with half of the sushi rice, and shape into nigiri sushi. Make another piece with the squid and rice. Garnish with Dry Miso and serve.

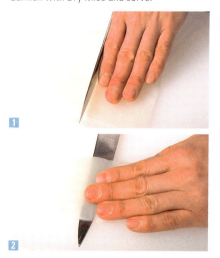

NIGIRI SUSHI

FLASH-BLANCHED SQUID NIGIRI WITH JALAPEÑO SALSA

This dish uses a technique called *yushimo*, which is to cook just the outside of something, changing its color to a frosty white with hot water. This helps to bring out the sweetness of the squid and the beautiful appearance of a pinecone. Jalapeño salsa adds a unique flavor not found in the Japanese flavor palette.

MAKES 2 PIECES

generous 2 tablespoons (30 grams) sushi rice

1 sashimi-grade squid body, cleaned and butterflied (PAGE 159)

2 teaspoons Jalapeño Salsa (PAGE 151)

soy sauce for dipping

Cut the squid body in half and finely score (at 1/10-inch/1- to 2-mm intervals) the outer side of one squid piece in a diagonal crosshatch pattern.

Prepare a pot of boiling water and a bowl of ice-cold water. Blanch the squid for about 5 seconds and immediately transfer to ice-cold water to cool. Drain and blot dry. Cut off two 1×3-inch (2.5×7.5-cm) pieces.

Place one squid piece on the fingers of your left hand, scored side down. Lay half of the sushi rice on the squid and shape into nigiri. Repeat with the second piece. Arrange both nigiri pieces on a serving plate. Garnish with Jalapeño Salsa and serve with soy sauce.

NIGIRI SUSHI

BOILED PRAWN WITH EGG YOLK CRUMBLES NIGIRI

Hard-boiled egg yolks are cooked with sweet vinegar and then pushed through a fine strainer to create bright yellow crumbles, called *oboro* in Japanese. Boiled prawns are marinated in the crumbles to add a soft umami and gentle acidity to the prawn for a delicious combination. This technique has a long history and is a taste of tradition.

MAKES 2 PIECES

generous 2 tablespoons (30 grams) sushi rice
2 Boiled Japanese Tiger Prawns (PAGE 148)

Egg York Crumbles
- 2 hard-boiled egg yolks
- 2 tablespoons rice vinegar
- 1 tablespoon sugar

grated wasabi
soy sauce for dipping

Egg York Crumbles: Place the egg yolks in a saucepan over low heat. Holding 4 or 5 chopsticks in one hand, break up the egg yolks into fine crumbles and stir to dry. Combine the rice vinegar and sugar in a bowl and mix until the sugar is dissolved. Add the sweetened vinegar to the egg yolks and keep stirring (PHOTO 1). When the egg yolks become dry and fluffy, remove from heat and let cool. With a wooden spatula, push the egg yolks through a fine mesh sieve to make fine crumbles (PHOTO 2). Egg Yolk Crumbles will keep for up to 2 days refrigerated in a clean container.

Remove the head and shells (keep tails attached) from the boiled prawns. Slit the belly side open and devein. Put in the container with the Egg Yolk Crumbles to coat and refrigerate overnight.

To make nigiri: Place one egg-crumble-coated prawn on the fingers of your left hand, outer side down. Spread some wasabi on the prawn, top with half of the sushi rice, and shape into nigiri sushi. Repeat with the second prawn. Garnish with a small amount of Egg Yolk Crumbles on top and serve with soy sauce.

NIGIRI SUSHI

NORTH PACIFIC OCTOPUS NIGIRI

Fresh North Pacific octopus, harvested in the cold waters of Hokkaido and the coast of North America, is a variety of very large octopus known for its elastic texture. This octopus can be eaten raw. This is topped with flavorful and umami-rich Dry Miso.

MAKES 1 PIECE

generous 1 tablespoon (15 grams) sushi rice
1 slice sashimi-grade North Pacific Octopus (PAGE 159)
grated wasabi
Dry Miso (PAGE 168)

To make the texture softer, cut several small incisions on one side of the octopus slice.

Place the octopus slice on the fingers of your left hand, scored side down. Spread some wasabi on the octopus, top with the sushi rice, and shape into nigiri sushi. Garnish with Dry Miso.

RED BEAN-INFUSED OCTOPUS NIGIRI

The colorful Japanese name of the cooked octopus, *sakurani*, comes from the cherry blossom pink color after the octopus legs have been simmered. By simmering the legs with azuki red beans, not only does this gentle color develop, but also the octopus meat softens. Instead of soy sauce, some of the reduction from the pan is brushed over the octopus.

MAKES 1 PIECE

generous 1 tablespoon (15 grams) sushi rice

Red Bean-Infused Octopus and Reduction Sauce
- 1 live octopus, cleaned (PAGE 158)
- 2 cups (500 ml) water
- 2 tablespoons dried azuki red beans
- generous 2 tablespoons sugar, preferably *wasanbon* sugar (alternatively granulated sugar)
- scant 2 teaspoons salt

grated wasabi

Red Bean-Infused Octopus: Combine water, azuki red beans, sugar, and salt in a saucepan and bring to a boil over high heat. Cook until the color of the water turns pinkish.

Slowly submerge the octopus in boiling stock from the tip of its legs so that the legs will curl beautifully. Bring the stock back to a boil, turn the heat to low and simmer for about 2 hours. Keep the heat low to prevent the flesh from becoming tough. Gently take out the octopus and let cool. The Cooked octopus will keep for 3 days refrigerated.

Reduction Sauce: Strain the stock from the beans and return the liquid to the saucepan. Cook until the liquid becomes a thick syrup, continuously stirring and scraping the bottom of the pan with a wooden spatula to prevent it from burning. Remove from heat just before it reaches the desired consistency, since it will thicken as it cools. The sauce will keep for 2 to 3 weeks refrigerated.

To make nigiri: Cut the octopus legs from the body and reserve the head for another purpose. Place one of the cut legs on the cutting board and cut off a slice from the thick part. Insert the blade of your knife at the appropriate angle to produce a slice, which will be about 1/5 inch (5–6 mm) thick and 3 inches (7.5 cm) long.

Place the octopus slice on the fingers of your left hand. Spread some wasabi on the octopus, top with the sushi rice, and shape into nigiri sushi. Brush some Reduction Sauce on top and serve.

NOTE

Boiled octopus is often sliced in a method called *namigata*, which resembles waves or corrugated cardboard on the flesh. Not only does this make the appearance more beautiful but it also prevents the octopus slice from slipping off of the sushi rice and keeps the sauce from dripping off.

Cut into the boiled octopus changing the angle little by little from horizontal to vertical. The finished cut should look like ripples or little waves.

SAKÉ-FLAVORED SCALLOP NIGIRI

Cooking sashimi-quality scallops in hot saké brings out the natural sweetness in the shellfish. The scallops are warmed through but not cooked through. The soft and mellow scallop is countered by the crunchy and refreshing *Charaquita* Salsa.

MAKES 2 PIECES

generous 2 tablespoons (30 grams) sushi rice

2 sashimi-grade scallops

saké

2 teaspoons *Charaquita* Salsa (PAGE 151)

grated wasabi

soy sauce for dipping

Place enough saké in a small saucepan that will fully cover the scallops. Bring the saké to a boil and add the scallops to cook for about 5 seconds or until the surface color just changes. Do not cook all the way through. Immediately transfer to ice-cold water to cool. Drain and blot dry. Discard the saké.

    Butterfly a scallop by laterally inserting the knife blade up to the middle of the scallop. Place one scallop on the fingers of your left hand, cut-side up. Spread some wasabi on the scallop, top with half of the sushi rice, and shape into nigiri sushi. Repeat with the second scallop. Arrange both nigiri pieces on a servng plate. Garnish with *Charaquita* Salsa and serve with soy sauce.

FLASH-SEARED *HOKKIGAI* CLAM NIGIRI

Hokkigai clams are celebrated for being juicy, sweet, and having a unique crunchy texture. While a *hokkigai* clam can also be eaten raw, just a little bit of heat will help increase its umami and sweetness.

MAKES 2 PIECES

generous 2 tablespoons (30 grams) sushi rice

1 sashimi-grade *hokkigai* clam, blanched and cleaned (PAGE 160)

grated wasabi

soy sauce for dipping

Cut the *hokkigai* clam in half to make 2 symmetrical pieces. Make several scores across the outer side of both pieces. Sear over a preheated *yakiami* grill on the scored side for 3 to 5 seconds. Be careful not to overcook the clam so as not to lose the treasured texture.

    Place one piece of *hokkigai* clam on the fingers of your left hand, seared side down. Spread some wasabi on the clam, top with half of the sushi rice, and shape into nigiri sushi. Repeat with the second piece. Serve with soy sauce.

NIGIRI SUSHI

SIMMERED *ANAGO* EEL NIGIRI

Soft and tender simmered *anago* eel is an essential member of traditional Edo-style sushi. It is briefly seared just before making into nigiri sushi to add some toasty notes. The sushi rice falls apart in your mouth, while the delicate *anago* melts. Garnish with the reduction sauce for a richer dish or with sea salt flakes for a lighter version.

MAKES 2 PIECES

generous 2 tablespoons (30 grams) sushi rice

2 slices Simmered *Anago* Eel (PAGE 150)

grated wasabi

sea salt flakes, such as Maldon sea salt or fleur de sel

Anago Broth Reduction (PAGE 150)

Sear the skin side only of the Simmered *Anago* Eel slices on a preheated *yakiami* grill or cook in a toaster oven until browned.

　Place one slice of *anago* on the fingers of your left hand, seared side down. Spread some wasabi on the fish, top with half of the sushi rice, and shape into nigiri sushi. Repeat with the second slice. Arrange both nigiri pieces on a serving plate. Place sea salt flakes on one piece and brush some *Anago* Broth Reduction on the other.

HAKUNI-STYLE SIMMERED ANAGO EEL NIGIRI

Anago eel can be simmered in a style that preserves its natural white color (*hakuni*, literally "white-simmered"). Light-colored soy sauce, salt, and saké are the main components in the simmering broth that produces the unadulterated flavor of *anago* eel.

MAKES 2 PIECES

generous 2 tablespoons (30 grams) sushi rice

Light-Colored Soy-Simmered *Anago* Eel

2 to 3 fresh *anago* eels, butterflied

2 cups (500 ml) water

scant ¼ cup (50 ml) saké

1½ tablespoons granulated sugar

1 tablespoon light-colored soy sauce (*usukuchi shōyu*)

½ teaspoon salt

Reduction Sauce

2 cups (500 ml) Basic *Dashi* Stock (PAGE 113)

scant ¼ cup (50 ml) soy sauce

scant ¼ cup (50 ml) mirin

scant ¼ cup (50 ml) saké

4 tablespoons granulated sugar

1 knob ginger

grated wasabi

Shōyu-Jio (PAGE 169)

Light-Colored Soy-Simmered *Anago* Eel (yields 2 to 3 whole *anago*, of which 2 slices (1 ounce/30 grams) are used for this dish): Clean and rinse the slimy skin of the *anago* eel (see recipe for Simmered *Anago* Eel; PAGE 150). Combine water, saké, granulated sugar, light-colored soy sauce, and salt in a large saucepan and bring to a boil over high heat. Add the *anago* eels, one by one, to the boiling liquid. When it returns to a boil, lower the heat and simmer for 8 minutes. The cooked *anago* will keep up to 3 days refrigerated.

Reduction Sauce: Combine all the ingredients in a saucepan and boil over high heat until the liquid becomes a thick syrup, continuously stirring and scraping the bottom of the pan with a wooden spatula to prevent it from burning. Remove from heat just before it reaches the desired consistency, since it will thicken a bit as it cools. The sauce will keep for up to 1 month refrigerated.

To make nigiri: Cut off 2 *anago* eel slices. Place one piece of fish on the fingers of your left hand, skin side down. Spread some wasabi on the *anago*, top with half of the sushi rice, and shape into nigiri sushi. Repeat with the second piece. Arrange both pieces on a serving plate. Brush some Reduction Sauce on one piece and place *Shōyu-Jio* on the other.

DASHIMAKI OMELET WITH SEA URCHIN NIGIRI

Dashi stock and other ingredients are added to beaten eggs then cooked in a special Japanese omelet pan (*tamagoyaki nabé*). The cooked egg is gently rolled onto itself to make a succulent *dashimaki* omelet. In this version, steamed sea urchin is added between the layers.

MAKES 2 PIECES

generous 2 tablespoons (30 grams) sushi rice

Dashimaki Omelet with Sea Urchin, for 1 roll using 10 × 10 × 2-inch (24.5 × 24.5 × 5-cm) square Japanese omelet pan

- 5 eggs
- 5 tablespoons Basic *Dashi* Stock (PAGE 113), cooled to room temperature
- ½ teaspoon light-colored soy sauce (*usukuchi shōyu*)
- 3 tablespoons granulated sugar
- pinch of salt
- 2 ounces (60 grams) sashimi-grade sea urchin (*uni*)
- vegetable oil for frying

soy sauce for dipping

Dashimaki Omelet with Sea Urchin: Spread the sea urchin in a single layer in a small cooking tray or a plate and steam in a steamer for 3 to 4 minutes. Remove from the steamer and cool.

Crack the eggs into a bowl and add the Basic *Dashi* Stock, soy sauce, sugar, and salt. Beat gently; try to liquefy the viscous egg whites without incorporating too much air.

Heat a square (or rectangular) Japanese omelet pan over medium heat. Take a small piece of paper towel dipped in vegetable oil and coat the entire surface of the pan lightly with oil. Be especially careful about oiling the corners. When the pan is ready, pour in one-third of the egg mixture. Tilt and rotate the pan to spread the mixture evenly into every corner, breaking air bubbles formed on the surface (PHOTO 1). When the egg mixture is almost set, lay half of the steamed sea urchin crosswise on the far edge of the omelet (about 1 inch/2.5 cm from the far edge) (PHOTO 2). Tilt the far end of the pan up towards you. With chopsticks or a spatula gently roll the egg layer towards you, covering the sea urchin.

Gently slide the roll with chopsticks or a spatula to the far end

of the pan away from you, and recoat the pan with the oiled paper towel. Pour in half of the remaining egg mixture (one-third of the original amount) and spread; lift the roll and introduce the fresh egg mixture underneath the omelet (PHOTO 3). Scatter half of the remaining sea urchin (a quarter of the original amount) on the egg mixture and roll towards you (PHOTO 4). Repeat once more with the remaining egg mixture and sea urchin.

This omelet will keep for up to 2 days tightly wrapped in plastic wrap and refrigerated.

To make nigiri: Cut off two generous 4×1×½-inch (10×3×1-cm; 1-ounce/35-gram) slices from one side of the egg. If it is hard to integrate simply sliced omelet over sushi rice, use the *namigata* technique (PAGE 84 NOTE) when slicing the omelet.

Place a slice of omelet on the fingers of your left hand, top with half of the sushi rice, and shape into nigiri sushi. Repeat with the second slice. Serve with soy sauce.

THICK BAKED OMELET WITH FISH AND SHRIMP PASTE

The Tokyo-style of thick omelet is made with a white fish and shrimp paste (PAGE 149) and is very flavorful. It can be used as a topping for sushi or served on its own as a side dish for saké. Here a branding iron is heated up until it is red hot and then pressed onto the omelet. The sugar in the omelet caramelizes, and the result is this NOBU stamp.

Slice the omelet into 1×3-inch (2.5×7.5-cm) pieces. Serve with soy sauce.

GUNKAN SUSHI WITH THREE TOPPINGS

Gunkan sushi is a technique that was invented as a way to serve sushi made from loose toppings like sea urchin or salmon roe. Form the sushi rice as you would if you are making nigiri sushi. Then using a long, narrow piece of nori, make a collar and wrap it around the rice. Fill with toppings like minced fatty tuna, sea urchin, shredded snow crab leg meat, and caviar for a refined sushi.

MAKES 3 PIECES

scant ¼ cup (45 grams) sushi rice

½ sheet nori

grated wasabi

1 slice or scant ½ ounce (12 grams) sashimi-grade medium fatty tuna (*chūtoro*), minced

1 to 2 teaspoons sashimi-grade sea urchin (*uni*)

meat of 1 boiled snow crab leg, shredded

3 teaspoons caviar

soy sauce for dipping

To cut nori for *gunkan* sushi, place the halved nori on the cutting board with length facing away. Trim 1 inch (3 cm) off the bottom of the nori. Divide the remaining piece into three long strips.

TO MAKE *GUNKAN* SUSHI:

1 Divide the sushi rice into 3 parts and shape 3 nigiri rice forms. Place one of the nigiri on a cutting board.

2 Take a strip of nori and form a collar with it around one nigiri.

3 To help the nori stick to the rice, begin by placing one end of the nori slightly higher as you wind, bringing the nori edge level with the cutting board. When you finish, the first edge will stick up slightly.

4 Repeat with the remaining nigiri rice forms.

5 Spread some wasabi over the rice. Place either minced tuna, sea urchin, or shredded snow crab leg meat on each piece. Add a dab of caviar and serve with soy sauce.

HOME ENTERTAINING SUSHI PARTY IDEAS

Colorful and beautiful, bite-sized nigiri sushi is the original finger food. It can be paired with champagne as an appetizer, with saké as the main course of a meal, or as the highlight of a party.

As part of *omoténashi*, the Japanese art of hospitality and sensibilities of service when entertaining guests, the host plans a menu that will not only be beautiful to look at, but will also be easy for the guest to eat. Nobu shares a few tips on how to make NOBU-Style presentations.

Sasamaki, Sushi in Bamboo Leaf Cones

The first sushi party idea I would like to introduce is to serve sushi in elegant and quintessentially Japanese *sasamaki*. Nigiri sushi is made with your favorite toppings (see PAGES 56–57) and then presented in fragrant *sasa* bamboo leaves folded into cones. The green *sasa* bamboo leaf is a lovely contrast to the colorful red tuna, crab legs, boiled prawn, white fish, or orange salmon, and creates a dramatic presentation.

Hold the *sasa* bamboo leaf cone, drizzle a bit of soy sauce over the nigiri, and eat the sushi as you peel open the leaf. The leaf itself is not consumed; it prevents hands and clothes from being soiled and has a fresh aroma. Aligned at an angle on a long, rectangular plate, the lovely presentation is very Japanese, and the sushi will be easy for your guests to pick up. I especially recommend this method for those still learning to make nigiri sushi. The *sasa* bamboo leaf cone helps to disguise any misshapen nigiri pieces.

Sasa bamboo leaves should be available at large Japanese markets or online and should be soaked in cold water before being used.

HOW TO MAKE A SASA BAMBOO LEAF CONE

1 | Wipe off excess water from a *sasa* bamboo leaf and hold it flat, stem side left.

2 | Bend the leaf, making the cone apex one-third the length from the stem end.

3 | Roll up tightly, making sure there is enough room inside.

4 | Fold in the tip of the leaf to fix.

Mini Sushi Cups

The second sushi party idea I would like to introduce is a modern presentation of sushi cups, which is a stark contrast to the traditional Japanese *sasamaki*. Filled with a colorful variety of toppings and arranged with taste, sushi cups will take center stage on any table. Depending on the toppings, either drizzle with soy sauce or not and eat with chopsticks or forks.

Mini sushi cups are easy to prepare. Place sushi rice in small cups and add wasabi as you like over the rice. Slice the toppings into bite-sized pieces and place over the sushi rice. Small saké cups are ideal, but any small cups, about 2 to 3 inches (5 to 7 cm) in diameter, will do. Since the sushi rice and toppings don't need to be formed into a nigiri, this variation could not be easier. You can use toppings as shown, like octopus, sea urchin, eel, salmon, fish roe, avocado, Vinegared Mackerel, or thinly julienned squid. I also like Kombu-Cured Vegetables (PAGES 100, 124) as toppings, which are unique and add variety, like a salad. Think about a variety of colors when selecting your toppings to make a colorful and impressive presentation.

SUSHI BOWLS AND BOX-PRESSED SUSHI

Chirashi-Zushi / Oshi-Zushi

Chirashi-zushi is sometimes translated as "scattered sushi." Fresh seafood, vegetables, simmered dried foods, julienned thin omelet, and more are artistically placed on sushi rice for a colorful dish. Box-pressed sushi is made using a *oshi-zushi* box mold to layer sushi rice and other ingredients, which are then pressed. Compared to sushi rolls or nigiri sushi, these are simple techniques, and assembly is easy.

KOMBU-CURED VEGETABLES SUSHI BOWL (see PAGE 100 for recipe)

KOMBU-CURED VEGETABLES SUSHI BOWL

The vivid colors and beautiful natural shapes and flavors of vegetables can be enjoyed when simply cured with kombu. Vegetables sandwiched between kombu sheets and left to rest become rich in umami.

SERVES 1

1 cup (150 grams) sushi rice

Kombu-Cured Vegetables

- 2 large kombu sheets, preferably Rausu kombu
- 1 to 2 tablespoons saké
- 4 to 5 stalks baby asparagus, blanched in salted water
- 3 ounces (90 grams) vegetables that can be eaten raw, such as zucchini, baby radish, baby carrot, Japanese turnip (*kabu*), or roseheart radish, cut into ¼-inch (5-to-6-mm) thick slices
- salt

⅙ avocado, cut into bite-sized pieces

½ sheet nori, julienned

kinomé sprigs, *hana hojiso* (PAGE 168) stalks, and a thin curl of daikon for optional garnishes

soy sauce, optional

Dampen a small piece of paper towel with saké and lightly wipe the kombu sheets to soften them.

Sprinkle a little salt evenly on a large cooking tray. Arrange the blanched asparagus and other raw vegetables for Kombu-Cured Vegetables in one layer over the salt. Lightly sprinkle the vegetables with salt and let rest for 5 minutes. When the vegetables start to sweat, transfer them onto one of the softened kombu sheets. Place the second kombu sheet over the vegetables. Tightly cover with plastic wrap and refrigerate overnight or for 12 hours.

Place the sushi rice in a serving bowl and gently flatten its surface. Scatter the julienned nori over the rice. Arrange the avocado pieces and Kombu-Cured Vegetables over the nori. Garnish with *kinomé*, *hana hojiso*, and a daikon curl. Serve with soy sauce if needed.

NOTE

Kombu sheets can be used for curing vegetables 4 to 5 times if wiped with a saké-dampened cloth and dried thoroughly after each use.

SUSHI BOWLS AND BOX-PRESSED SUSHI

FLASH-SEARED SEAFOOD SUSHI BOWL

Just before serving, sashimi or other cooked seafood is lightly seared and placed over sushi rice. The seafood is slightly warm and has a toasty aroma, offering a different flavor profile from raw seafood. Freshly ground pepper spices up the dish.

SERVES 1

1 cup (150 grams) sushi rice

about 8 pieces of various sashimi-grade seafood, such as squid (PAGE 159), *akagai* clam (PAGE 160), scallops, boiled snow crab leg meat, *hamachi* yellowtail, medium-fatty tuna (*chūtoro*), Boiled Japanese Tiger Prawn (head and shells removed, PAGE 148), Simmered *Anago* Eel (PAGE 150), and Vinegared Mackerel (PAGE 75)

salt

black pepper, freshly ground

½ sheet nori, julienned

Julienned Thin Omelet (PAGE 149)

gari pickled ginger, cut into bite-sized pieces

kinomé sprigs

soy sauce, optional

Finely score the outer side of the squid in a crosshatch pattern (see PAGE 81). Sprinkle salt and pepper on each side of all the sashimi pieces, and sear over a preheated *yakiami* grill on one side only (scored side for the squid and flesh side for the Simmered *Anago* Eel) for 3 seconds or until they are lightly marked. Cut into bite-sized pieces.

Place the sushi rice in a serving bowl and gently flatten its surface. Layer the sushi rice first with shredded nori and then with the Julienned Thin Omelet. Arrange the seared sashimi, *gari* pickled ginger, and *kinomé*. Serve with soy sauce if needed.

NOBU-STYLE CEVICHE SUSHI BOWL

Abalone and scallops are part of this deluxe ceviche, one of NOBU's signature dishes. The seafood is marinated for a short period in a citrus-based sauce to showcase its freshness and highlight its aroma. This ceviche is also delicious over sushi rice.

SERVES 1

1 cup (150 grams) sushi rice

1 live abalone with shell, 7 to 10 ounces (200 to 300 grams)

2-inch (5-cm) square kombu

pinch of salt

1 Boiled Japanese Tiger Prawn (PAGE 148), head and shell removed

1 sashimi-grade scallop

⅔ ounce (20 grams) of sashimi-grade North Pacific Octopus (PAGE 159), flounder (*hiramé*), and salmon, or other mild-flavored seafood

½ Japanese cucumber or ¼ English cucumber

¼ red onion

½ tomato

2 teaspoons Ceviche Sauce (PAGE 151)

1 tablespoon chopped coriander leaves

Shucking and steaming abalone: Clean the abalone by scrubbing it with a stiff brush. Rinse thoroughly. Hold the abalone with the shell down, insert a large, flat spoon under the flesh, and gently scrape to dislodge the flesh from the shell. Remove the black-colored internal organs attached to the flesh and discard. Place the abalone in a small heat-resistant container. Add salt, kombu, and water until it just covers the abalone. Tightly wrap the container first with plastic wrap and then with aluminum foil. Steam in a steamer for 2 to 3 hours or until the abalone is tender. Reserve about quarter of the flesh for the ceviche.

    Cut the reserved abalone, Boiled Japanese Tiger Prawn, scallop, North Pacific Octopus, flounder, salmon, cucumber, onion, and tomato into bite-sized pieces. Place in a medium-sized bowl and dress with Ceviche Sauce. Mix in chopped coriander leaves. This should be done just before serving in order to keep the fresh flavor and texture of the seafood.

    Place the sushi rice in a serving bowl and gently flatten its surface. Arrange the ceviche over the sushi rice. Drizzle any remaining sauce in the bowl over the seafood and serve.

NOBU-STYLE 4

CEVICHE

Influenced by his time in Peru and Argentina, Nobu's cuisine reflects the flavors and colors of South America. Ceviche is one of these dishes and is popular at NOBU restaurants around the world. In the original Peruvian version, the seafood is marinated for hours until the flesh turns opaque white. But at NOBU, super-fresh seafood is used and should be eaten to appreciate the quality; this ceviche is quickly dressed in the marinade just before serving.

SUSHI BOWLS AND BOX-PRESSED SUSHI

TRADITIONAL *CHIRASHI* SUSHI BOWL

This sushi is served on many occasions and celebrations at homes in Japan. All of the ingredients are traditional, and there is no raw seafood. Chicken with root and dried vegetables produce a variety of flavors that come together harmoniously to complete this dish.

SERVES 4

4 cups (600 grams) sushi rice

Seasoned Chicken and Root Vegetables

- 5 ounces (150 grams) chicken thigh meat with skin
- ½ burdock root (2½ ounces/75 grams)
- 4-inch (10-cm) length lotus root, peeled
- 1 boiled bamboo shoot, approximately 8 ounces (250 grams)
- ½ carrot (4 ounces/120 grams), peeled
- 1 cup (250 ml) Basic *Dashi* Stock (PAGE 113)
- 2⅔ tablespoons mirin
- 2⅔ tablespoons soy sauce

saké

3 Soy-Simmered Shiitaké Mushrooms (PAGE 148), blotted dry

about 3-foot length (⅔ ounce/20 grams) Soy-Simmered *Kampyō* (PAGE 150), blotted dry

Julienned Thin Omelet (PAGE 149)

8 ginkgo nuts, toasted and shells removed

mitsuba (trefoil), cut into ½-inch (1.5-cm) lengths

Seasoned Chicken and Root Vegetables: Rinse the burdock root just before using. Hold it under cold running water, scrubbing well with a stiff brush to remove any soil, or scrape off the outer layer of the root. The back of a knife also works well. Cut or slice the burdock root into bite-sized pieces and immediately place in cold water to minimize discoloration.

Cut the chicken, lotus root, and bamboo shoot into bite-sized pieces. Julienne the carrot.

Put the Basic *Dashi* Stock, mirin, and soy sauce in a saucepan and bring to a boil over high heat. Add the chicken, burdock root, lotus root, bamboo shoot, and carrot. Bring back to a boil. Lower the heat and simmer for 10 to 15 minutes or until the ingredients are tender (PHOTO 1). Remove from heat, allow to cool, and drain.

Cut Soy-Simmered Shiitake Mushrooms and Soy-Simmered *Kampyō* into the same size as the root vegetables.

Fold the seasoned chicken, root vegetables, shiitaké mushrooms, and *kampyō* into the sushi rice (PHOTO 2). Divide the rice mixture into serving bowls. Garnish with Julienned Thin Omelet, ginkgo nuts, and *mitsuba*.

NOTE

If you can't find all of the ingredients at your Asian market, just make the dish with what you can find.

SUSHI BOWLS AND BOX-PRESSED SUSHI

BOX-PRESSED *UNAGI* EEL SUSHI

The history of box-pressed sushi precedes Edo Tokyo-style nigiri sushi. This is the main style of sushi found in the Kansai region (greater Kyoto-Osaka). Vacuum-pouched *unagi* eel is convenient for putting together this sushi; aromatic dried chrysanthemum petals make it a colorful and impressive dish.

MAKES ONE 7¼×3⅝×2-INCH (18×9×5-CM) BOX-PRESSED SUSHI; 6 PIECES

1⅓ cup (250 grams) sushi rice
1 glaze-grilled *unagi* eel, vacuum-pouched
1 sheet *hoshigiku* (dried chrysanthemum petals)
grated wasabi
soy sauce for dipping

Reheat the glaze-grilled eel either by submerging the sealed pouch in a hot water bath or by directly grilling or broiling the eel. Allow the eel to cool to room temperature and cut into the same size as the mold's frame. Cut the *hoshigiku* sheet into the same size. Feel free to mix some of the glaze sauce that is included with the grilled eel into the sushi rice.

Lightly dampen the inner surfaces of the *oshi-zushi* box mold (the frame and the two boards that are the top and bottom of the mold) with vinegar water to prevent the rice from sticking to the mold. Place the first board in the frame with the smooth side up. Place the eel on the board, skin side up, and spread some wasabi over the eel. Place half of the rice on the eel and gently flatten (PHOTO 1). Layer with the *hoshigiku* sheet and then the other half of the rice (PHOTO 2). Place the second board with the smooth side facing the rice, and press firmly.

Turn the whole mold upside down so that the eel is on top. Hold the top board with both thumbs and remove the frame by pulling it up with your other fingers, as shown in PHOTO 3 and PHOTO 4. Remove the top board and cut the sushi into 6 pieces while still on the bottom board. Slice with a sharp knife, wiping the blade with a damp cloth after each cut. Transfer to a plate and serve with soy sauce.

NOTE

- You can use other common toppings for box-pressed sushi, such as Simmered *Anago* Eel (PAGE 150), Vinegared Mackerel (PAGE 75), vinegared sea bream, smoked salmon, and more.
- *Hoshigiku* can be substituted with finely julienned ginger or green *shiso* leaves. If you are able to obtain fresh edible chrysanthemums (PAGES 116, 167), pluck the petals, lightly blanch in boiling water, drain, let cool, and squeeze lightly to remove excess water.

BOX-PRESSED CUCUMBER SUSHI

The *oshi-zushi* mold is also convenient for making pressed sushi rice in a rectangular shape.

Add some condiments to sushi rice, press in the mold, cut into bite-sized pieces, and wrap with nori to serve a quick snack.

MAKES ONE 6×2⅓×2-INCH (16×6×5-CM) BOX-PRESSED SUSHI; 6 PIECES

generous 1 cup (200 grams) sushi rice
3 full sheets nori, cut in half lengthwise
1 Salt-Wilted Cucumber (PAGE 29)
1 teaspoon minced *myōga*
1 teaspoon minced ginger
1 teaspoon minced green *shiso* leaves
1 tablespoon toasted white sesame seeds

Soak the Salt-Wilted Cucumber in water for about 10 minutes to reduce the salinity. Squeeze the cucumber to remove any excess water and slice thinly. Mix the sushi rice, sliced cucumber, minced *myōga*, ginger, *shiso* leaves, and sesame seeds in a bowl.

Lightly wet the inner surfaces of the *oshi-zushi* box mold (the frame and top and bottom boards) with vinegar water to prevent the rice from sticking to the mold. Place the first board in the frame with the smooth side up. Put the rice mixture into the mold, lightly flatten, place the second board with the smooth side facing the rice, and press firmly.

Hold the top board with both thumbs and remove the frame by pulling it up with the other fingers (PAGE 108 PHOTOS 3–4). Remove the top board and cut the sushi into 6 pieces while still on the bottom board. Slice with a sharp knife, wiping the blade with a damp cloth after each cut. Since the nori loses its crispness quickly, wrap each piece of rice with nori just before serving. The rough side of the nori should face the rice.

SUSHI BOWLS AND BOX-PRESSED SUSHI

NOBU-STYLE SOUPS

In Japan, soups are often served with sushi. Soups are a thoughtful way to share seasonal ingredients in a Japanese style and can help to complete a meal when serving sushi.

BASIC *DASHI* STOCK
(KOMBU AND *KATSUOBUSHI* STOCK)

MAKES 1 QUART (1 LITER)

20 to 25 square inches (10 grams) kombu, preferably Rausu kombu

scant 2 ounces (50 grams) *katsuobushi*

5 cups (1.2 liters) water

1 Combine the kombu and the water in a medium-sized saucepan and place over high heat.

2 When the liquid reaches 175°F (80°C), or when some small bubbles appear around the edge, remove the kombu and turn off the heat.

3 Add the *katsuobushi* and allow it to fully submerge in the liquid. Wait for the flakes to sink to the bottom of the pan, which should take about 5 to 10 minutes.

4 Prepare to strain the stock. Put two layers of cheesecloth on a strainer and place over a bowl. If you have a second strainer of the same size, place it over the cheesecloth, since this will make straining easier.

5 Pour the stock through the lined strainer to remove the *katsuobushi*. Do not touch or squeeze the flakes left in the strainer, or the stock may taste fishy.

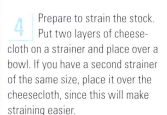

SPICY SEAFOOD SOUP

Scallops, squid, octopus, and other fresh seafood contribute to the broth of this spicy soup, which is very popular at NOBU restaurants. The seafood stock and spice helps to stimulate the appetite.

SERVES 4

Clear Soup

2½ cups (600 ml) Basic *Dashi* Stock (see LEFT)

scant 1 teaspoon salt

⅔ teaspoon light-colored soy sauce (*usukuchi shōyu*)

scant ½ teaspoon mirin

scant ½ teaspoon saké

12 live *asari* clams

4 fresh scallops

8 fresh squid legs

8 slices fresh octopus

4 fresh shrimp, head, tail, and shell attached

Chinese chili garlic paste (store-bought), to taste

mitsuba (trefoil), cut into ½-inch (1.5-cm) lengths

Rinse the *asari* clams well with water and place in a bowl. Cover with 3% salted water, which is about the same salinity as seawater. The basic ratio is about 2 cups (500 ml) water to 1 tablespoon of salt. Cover the bowl with plastic wrap and refrigerate overnight. The clams should expel any sand during this process.

Cut the scallops, squid legs, and octopus into bite-sized pieces. Remove the head, tail, and shell of the shrimp and devein. Bring a moderate amount of water to a boil and briefly blanch the scallops, squid legs, octopus, and shrimp in that order. Blanch just until the surface turns frosty white. Immediately transfer to a bowl of ice-cold water to cool and then drain. This will ensure a clearer finished soup.

Drain and rinse the clams. Combine the ingredients for the Clear Soup and clams in a saucepan. Bring to a boil over high heat. When the shells open, remove any scum. Add the scallops, squid legs, octopus, and shrimp. Turn off the heat as soon as it comes back to a boil. Add Chinese chili garlic paste. Pour in serving bowls and garnish with *mitsuba*.

NOTE

If seafood is cooked too long it will become tough, so simply heat until just cooked through and serve immediately.

for SPRING

SOUP WITH BABY SEA BREAM AND SOBA NOODLES

Kasugo-dai literally translates as "baby sea bream of spring." Harvested in the waters near Japan in March and April, this tiny sea bream is only about 3 inches (7.5 cm) in length. The scales sparkle and are the color of cherry blossoms, which bloom in the springtime. The delicate white flesh is lovely when served with soba noodles. Garnish with a salted cherry blossom, which floats in the soup and hints at the season.

SERVES 4

Clear Soup

- 2½ cups (600 ml) Basic *Dashi* Stock (PAGE 113)
- scant 1 teaspoon salt
- ⅔ teaspoon light-colored soy sauce (*usukuchi shōyu*)
- ⅔ teaspoon mirin
- ⅔ teaspoon saké

4 fillets fresh baby sea bream

3 ounces (80 grams) dried soba noodles

4 pieces kombu, each 3 inches (7.5 cm) square

4 salt-preserved cherry blossoms (see NOTE)

baby green *shiso* leaves

Bring a generous amount of water to a boil in a saucepan. Add the soba noodles and cook until al dente. Do not overcook. Drain in a strainer and wash off any starch on the soba with cold running water.

Place the baby sea bream fillets lengthwise, skin side down, on a working surface. Divide the soba into four portions and fold to about double the width of the sea bream fillets. Place each portion of soba across the middle of each sea bream fillet, roll up, and secure with a toothpick. Neatly trim both ends of the soba. Place the kombu pieces on a small cooking tray, set the sea bream rolls on top of each kombu piece, seam side down, and steam in a steamer for 4 to 5 minutes. Remove the toothpicks and keep warm.

Combine the ingredients of the Clear Soup in a saucepan and bring to a boil over high heat. Transfer the warm sea bream rolls with kombu in serving bowls. Pour in the Clear Soup and garnish with salt-pickled cherry blossoms and baby green *shiso* leaves.

NOTE

- Try to make the broth as clear as possible for this refined dish.
- Salt-preserved cherry blossoms are edible blossoms preserved in salt. They should be soaked in cold water to reduce salinity before being used.

for SUMMER

RED MISO SOUP WITH FRUIT TOMATO

Hatchō miso, native to the Nagoya region, is rich with umami and renowned for its distinctive flavor. This dark-colored, dense miso tastes wonderful, especially in the heat of summer. A very ripe, sweet tomato is the star of the simple and beautiful soup, and crunchy *hojiso* seedpods give an aromatic accent to the dish.

SERVES 4

2½ cups (600 ml) Basic *Dashi* Stock (PAGE 113)
generous 3 tablespoons Hatchō miso
4 small sweet tomatoes, preferably Japanese "fruit tomato"
2 sprigs *hojiso*, seedpods plucked from stem

Score the bottom of the tomatoes crosswise and hollow out the calyxes with the tip of a knife. Bring a generous amount of water to a boil. Submerge the tomatoes in boiling water for a few seconds and immediately transfer to a bowl of ice-cold water. Peel and discard the tomato skins. Place a tomato on the bottom of each serving bowl, bottom side up.

Bring the Basic *Dashi* Stock to a boil in a saucepan. Stir in the Hatchō miso and turn off the heat as soon as it comes back to a boil. Pour the soup over the tomatoes until halfway covered. Garnish with a scatter of *hojiso* seedpods.

CLEAR SOUP WITH CHRYSANTHEMUM PETALS

In Japan edible fresh chrysanthemum flowers come to the market in autumn. Here the petals are used in a simple but elegant soup. Diners pick up the lid from the soup bowl and are greeted with the gentle aroma of the chrysanthemum flowers and the lovely vision of petals, which appear to be dancing on the ripples of a stream.

SERVES 4

Clear Soup

2½ cups (600 ml) Basic *Dashi* Stock (PAGE 113)

scant 1 teaspoon salt

⅔ teaspoon light-colored soy sauce (*usukuchi shōyu*)

⅔ teaspoon mirin

⅔ teaspoon saké

4 fresh edible chrysanthemum flowers

Pluck the petals of the chrysanthemums, wash lightly in cold water, and drain well.

Combine the ingredients of the Clear Soup in a saucepan and bring to a boil. Pour into four serving bowls. Add the chrysanthemum petals, cover, and serve quickly.

KABURAMUSHI TURNIP SOUP

If you come across Japanese turnips in winter, try this festive dish to warm you up. The *kaburamushi* dumpling, made mainly with grated turnip and beaten egg whites, has a very soft texture that compliments the sea urchin and crab legs; the soup is lightly thickened with kuzu starch, which acts to hold the liquid's warmth.

SERVES 4

Clear Soup

- 2½ cups (600 ml) Basic *Dashi* Stock (PAGE 113)
- scant 1 teaspoon salt
- ⅔ teaspoon light-colored soy sauce (*usukuchi shōyu*)
- ⅔ teaspoon mirin
- ⅔ teaspoon saké

Kaburamushi

- 7 ounces (200 grams) grated and lightly drained Japanese turnip (*kabu*)
- 4 egg whites
- 4 teaspoons *katakuriko* (potato starch)
- 12 ginkgo nuts, toasted and shells removed
- meat of 8 boiled snow crab legs
- 4 tablespoons sashimi-grade sea urchin (*uni*)
- 4 teaspoons kuzu starch
- broccoli sprouts

Kaburamushi: Place the egg whites in a bowl and beat to stiff peaks. Place grated turnip in another bowl. Add the egg whites and *katakuriko* to the grated turnip and mix.

Divide the turnip mixture into 4 portions and form into small balls. Stuff each ball with 2 ginkgo nuts and 2 pieces of crab leg meat. Place the balls on a small cooking tray and place 1 tablespoon of sea urchin and 1 ginkgo nut on top of each ball. Steam the balls in a steamer for 5 to 8 minutes. Keep warm until ready to serve.

Combine the ingredients of the Clear Soup in a saucepan and bring to a boil. Mix the kuzu starch with 4 teaspoons of water in a bowl. Drizzle the mixture over the boiling soup while stirring continuously until it thickens a little.

Place one *kaburamushi* in each serving bowl and pour the thickened soup over. Garnish with broccoli sprouts.

NOTE

- Sweet, juicy, and tender Japanese turnips come into season in the cold winter months in Japan.
- The nut of the ginkgo tree comes in a stiff shell. The nut is yellow-jade green, has a chewy texture, and can be slightly bitter. It can sometimes be found in a shelled, ready-to-eat form in a vacuum pouch at Asian grocery stores.

Sushi, by nature, is the original finger food and is a perfect appetizer. To start a meal with a small bite accompanied by saké sets a festive mood.

A step away from traditional sushi, these recipes are fun and delicious. Sushi rice is formed into cubes and deep-fried or vegetables are used as serving dishes, etc. These colorful, bite-sized pieces allow guests to enjoy delicious appetizers while holding a drink in the other hand.

APPETI

APPETIZER SUSHI

CRISPY RICE CUBES WITH SPICY TUNA

It is no surprise that this is a popular appetizer at NOBU. Sushi rice is shaped in a *makisu*, pressed tight, then cut into cubes and deep-fried until golden brown and crisp. Spicy tuna tartar adds a contrasting texture and flavor.

MAKES 8 PIECES

generous ⅔ cup (130 grams) sushi rice
3 to 4 slices (1⅔ ounces/50 grams) sashimi-grade tuna
1 tablespoon chopped scallions or chives
1 tablespoon Spicy Mayonnaise Sauce (PAGE 151)
oil for deep-frying
soy sauce for dipping

Fully cover the *makisu* with plastic wrap. Dampen both hands with ice-cold water. Form the sushi rice into a log and set crosswise on the *makisu*. Adjust the rice log to fit the width of the *makisu*. Roll and shape the rice into a rectangular log 1×1×8 inches (2.5×2.5×20 cm). Tightly wrap the rice in plastic wrap and refrigerate overnight until firm.

    Just before deep-frying the rice, mince the tuna with a knife and put in a bowl. Add scallions and Spicy Mayonnaise Sauce and mix well.

    Cut the firm rice into 8 cubes (PHOTO 1). Skewer with bamboo skewers, preferably *matsuba-gushi*, pine needle-shaped bamboo skewers. Heat the oil to 350°F (180°C). Deep-fry the skewered rice cubes until evenly browned (PHOTO 2). Arrange the deep-fried rice cubes on a serving plate and spoon on some spicy tuna mixture. Serve with soy sauce.

NOTE

The rice cubes can be deep-fried ahead of time and garnished with the spicy tuna just before serving.

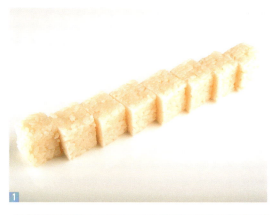

APPETIZER SUSHI

SUSHI "BON-BONS"

Don't mistake the ball-shaped sushi for bonbon candies. These attractive and easy to eat bite-sized pieces evoke an image of *témari*, Japanese traditional balls made with windings of colorful threads. Artfully arranged on a platter, these are sure to stand out on any table.

MAKES 12 PIECES

⅔ cup (120 grams) sushi rice

12 small slices (⅓ ounce/10 grams each) of your favorite sashimi-grade sushi toppings

green *shiso* leaves, cut into 6 or 8 pieces

grated wasabi

soy sauce for dipping

Place a slice of sushi topping on the center of a 8×8-inch (20×20-cm) plastic wrap. Spread some wasabi on the topping, add a piece of green *shiso* leaf if you like, and top with sushi rice that has been lightly hand-formed into a small ball (1 tablespoon/10 grams each) (PHOTO 1).

Gather the plastic wrap and twist tightly to form a small ball (PHOTO 2). Remove the plastic wrap and arrange on a serving plate. Use a new piece of plastic wrap for each ball. Serve with soy sauce.

APPETIZER SUSHI

VEGETABLE SUSHI

Colorful, kombu-cured vegetables rich in umami are the toppings for this sushi. This healthy and refreshing sushi can be served as a side dish to the main course, as a salad course, or as a meal when served with soup.

MAKES 12 PIECES

scant 1 cup (180 grams) sushi rice

Kombu-Cured Vegetables

- 2 large kombu sheets, preferably Rausu kombu
- 1 to 2 tablespoons saké
- 2 thin slices lotus root
- 1 leaf Chinese cabbage (*hakusai*)
- 1 to 2 thin slices vegetables for eating raw, such as Japanese turnip (*kabu*), roseheart radish, heirloom carrots, or zucchini
- salt

1 ounce (30 grams) énoki mushrooms

1 ounce (30 grams) *kaiwaré* daikon sprouts

3 thin slices avocado

1 slice *béttara-zuké* or other firm, not leafy Japanese pickled vegetable, ⅛ inch (4 mm) thick, finely scored in a crosshatch pattern

grated wasabi

soy sauce for dipping

Dampen a small piece of paper towel with saké and wipe the kombu sheets to soften them. If not using large kombu sheets, prepare several smaller pieces.

Blanch the lotus root in vinegar water. Blanch the Chinese cabbage in salted water, cool to room temperature, and squeeze to remove excess water. Sprinkle a little salt evenly in a large cooking tray. Arrange the lotus root, Chinese cabbage, and other vegetables for Kombu-Cured Vegetables in one layer on the salted tray. Lightly sprinkle the vegetables with salt and set aside for 5 minutes. When the vegetables start to sweat, transfer them onto a kombu sheet in one layer. Place the second kombu sheet over the vegetables. Tightly cover with plastic wrap and refrigerate overnight or for about 12 hours.

Bring a pot of salted water to a boil. Holding the base of the énoki mushrooms or the sponge attached to *kaiwaré* radish sprouts, put only the top part into the boiling water and blanch. Cool to room temperature. Squeeze to remove any excess water and cut off the base or sponge.

Cut the cured and other vegetables to a suitable size for the nigiri topping. Hold one portion with one hand and spread some wasabi on the vegetable. Top with rice (generous 1 tablespoon/15 grams each) and shape into nigiri sushi. See Basic Nigiri Hand-Forming Technique (PAGE 56). Serve with soy sauce.

Kombu sheets can be reused for curing vegetables 4 to 5 times if wiped with a saké-dampened cloth and dried thoroughly after each use. They can be reused for curing fish as well; however, once used for curing fish they should never be reused for curing vegetables.

NOTE

Béttara-zuké is a sweet and crisp pickle popular in Tokyo. Daikon is first brined and then pickled in a sweet *kōji* (PAGE 168) slurry. Here it is sliced into a bite-sized piece, and one side of the slice is finely scored in a crosshatch pattern (upper right).

APPETIZER SUSHI

SUSHI ON LETTUCE CUPS

The Traditional *Chirashi* Sushi (PAGE 106) can be served on lettuce leaves cut into rounds for a colorful bite-sized appetizer. The crunch and flavor of the lettuce is a nice contrast to the sushi. The refreshing dish is lovely, particularly when partnered with saké.

MAKES 8 PIECES

1 cup (150g) Traditional *Chirashi* Sushi (PAGE 106)

½ teaspoon minced *yuzu* peel, alternatively lemon or lime peel

1 teaspoon toasted white sesame seeds

8 leaves iceberg lettuce, cut in 4-inch (10-cm) diameter circles

Julienned Thin Omelet (PAGE 149)

mitsuba (trefoil), cut into ½-inch (1.5-cm) lengths

Mix together in a bowl Traditional *Chirashi* Sushi, minced *yuzu* peel, and sesame seeds.
 Arrange the lettuce cups on a serving plate. Divide the sushi into 8 portions and place on the lettuce cups. Garnish with Julienned Thin Omelet and *mitsuba*.

APPETIZER SUSHI

SUSHI WITH PICKLED *RAKKYŌ* ON RADICCHIO BOATS

Dark red radicchio leaves are the serving dish for this finger food. Sushi rice goes with pickled *rakkyō* bulbs, white fish sashimi, scallions, and *Shōyu-Jio*. On the palate there is bitterness in the radicchio, a delicate sweetness from the sashimi, as well as the acidity and bite from the pickled *rakkyō*.

MAKES 8 PIECES

⅔ cup (120 grams) sushi rice

2 pickled *rakkyō* bulbs, thinly sliced

8 radicchio leaves

3 to 4 slices (1⅔ ounces/50 grams) sashimi-grade, mild-flavored, white-fleshed fish such as sea bass (*suzuki*) or flounder (*hiramé*), cut into small pieces

chopped scallions or chives

Shōyu-Jio (PAGE 169)

Mix the sliced *rakkyō* bulbs with the sushi rice and divide into 8 parts. Form each part into a rice ball and place on the radicchio leaves. Place a couple pieces of fish on top. Garnish with scallions and *Shōyu-Jio*.

NOTE

Rakkyō is a Japanese ramp, a plant in the scallion family. Its small white-colored bulbs have a sharp flavor and a very intense aroma, which is similar to garlic or Chinese leeks. Often pickled in a sweet-and-sour marinade.

127

APPETIZER SUSHI

ARROZ CON POLLO (RICE WITH CHICKEN) IN A FREEZE-DRIED ONION CUP

This petite finger food packs a punch with flavor and in its presentation. The rice is cooked with chicken in beer, a traditional method from Peru. The unique freeze-dried vegetables are used for serving.

MAKES 8 PIECES

Arroz con Pollo

- 2¼ cups (450 grams) short-grain Japanese rice, washed, drained, and soaked (PAGE 12)
- 3 to 4 ounces (100 grams) boneless chicken thigh, cut into bite-sized pieces
- ⅓ ounce (10 grams) coriander leaves
- 1 clove garlic, sliced
- ½ teaspoon salt
- 2½ cups (600 ml) beer

8 pieces freeze-dried onion cups, store-bought (see NOTE)

The *Arroz con Pollo* recipe yields about 5 cups, of which ½ cup (80 grams) is used for this dish.

Arroz con Pollo: Place the rice, chicken, coriander leaves, garlic, and salt in a pot or an electric rice cooker. Reserve some coriander leaves for the garnish. Pour in the beer, cover, and cook the rice (PAGE 12). After the rice has been cooked, reserve some cooked chicken for the garnish and stir the remaining rice well.

Place about 1 tablespoon (10 grams) each of the cooked rice on the freeze-dried onion cups. Garnish with torn shreds of reserved chicken and coriander leaves.

NOTE

Germnon specializes in a variety of freeze-dried vegetables.
http://www.germnon.jp

APPETIZER SUSHI

TRICOLORED SUSHI ON FREEZE-DRIED BELL PEPPER SHELLS

Bell peppers are grilled over a direct flame to bring out their inherent sweetness. The peppers are then pureed and added to sushi rice to create a colorful, modern sushi.

MAKES 12 PIECES

scant 1 cup (180 grams) sushi rice

1 teaspoon each of green, yellow, and red bell pepper puree

4 pieces each of green, yellow, and red freeze-dried bell pepper shells, store-bought (PAGE 128 NOTE)

12 thin rounds jalapeño chili

Dry Miso (PAGE 168)

Bell pepper puree: Push a fork into a bell pepper and grill over a direct flame on the stove top until the skin is completely charred. Remove the skin and seeds. Puree in a food processor. Repeat the puree process for each color of bell pepper.

Divide the sushi rice into three parts. Add the green, yellow, and red bell pepper puree to each and mix well until the puree is incorporated and the rice has a colorful tint.

Make four nigiri rice forms from each color of rice and place on the bell pepper shells of the same color. Garnish with jalapeño chili and Dry Miso.

APPETIZER SUSHI

SUSHI SANDWICH WITH *MONAKA* WAFERS

Monaka, a popular Japanese confection, are delicate wafers made from Japanese sticky rice that are filled with sweet azuki bean paste. Here *monaka* wafers are used to sandwich the sushi filling, a fun finger food for any party.

MAKES 8 PIECES

⅔ cup (120 grams) sushi rice

8 pairs of *monaka* wafer shells, store-bought

2×2×2-inch (5×5×5-cm) piece Thick Baked Omelet (PAGE 149)

2 Boiled Japanese Tiger Prawns (PAGE 148), deveined, heads, tails, and shells removed

2 to 3 Soy-Simmered Shiitaké Mushrooms (PAGE 148)

1 ounce (30 grams) Soy-Simmered *Kampyō* (PAGE 150)

1⅔ ounces (50 grams) Vinegared Mackerel (PAGE 75)

2 green *shiso* leaves, minced

1 teaspoon *masago* roe

Cut Thick Baked Omelet, Boiled Japanese Tiger Prawns, Soy-Simmered Shiitaké Mushrooms, Soy-Simmered *Kampyō*, and Vinegared Mackerel into ½-inch (1-cm) cubes.

    Place the sushi rice in a bowl. Add the *shiso* leaves and *masago* roe and mix. Add the omelet, prawns, shiitaké mushroom, *kampyō*, and mackerel pieces and lightly mix. Divide into 8 parts.

    Place the rice mixture onto 8 *monaka* wafer shells. Cover with the remaining 8 wafer shells. Serve immediately while the wafers are still crisp.

130 APPETIZER SUSHI

APPETIZER SUSHI

WASABI LEAF-WRAPPED SUSHI

Did you know that the leaves of wasabi may also be used as an ingredient? Quickly blanched to soften the fibers and bring out the aroma, the leaves can be used as a wrapper for sushi rice. The sushi is garnished with a salsa-like Wasabi Mixture for a flavorful dish.

MAKES 8 PIECES

generous ⅔ cup (130 grams) sushi rice

Wasabi Mixture
- 1 ounce (30 grams) fresh wasabi, peeled and minced
- 2 ounces (60 grams) red onion, minced
- 1 teaspoon grapeseed oil
- ½ teaspoon grated garlic
- pinch of salt
- pinch of ground black pepper

3 to 5 wasabi leaves

salt

horseradish, to taste, peeled and julienned

soy sauce for dipping

Wasabi Mixture: Place the ingredients of the Wasabi Mixture in a bowl and mix well. Set aside.

Bring water to a boil. Add a pinch of salt and blanch the wasabi leaves. Plunge in cold water to cool and squeeze to remove any excess water. Lay out the leaves across the *makisu*, partly overlapping to create a sheet.

Dampen both hands with ice-cold water. Form the sushi rice into a log and set crosswise on the sheet of the leaves. Adjust the rice log to fit the width of the *makisu*. Roll and shape into a rectangular log. Remove the *makisu* and cut the roll into 8 pieces with a sharp knife, wiping the blade with a damp cloth after each cut.

Arrange the sushi on a serving plate, top with the Wasabi Mixture and julienned horseradish. Serve with soy sauce.

SAKÉ AND APERITIFS

Customers at NOBU restaurants often remark on the high quality of NOBU's saké and cocktails. The concept of NOBU is to promote Japanese food and beverage culture throughout the world with delicious sushi and beverages. Here, Nobu shares his thoughts on enjoying saké.

Saké is a natural partner for Japanese cuisine. What I look for when selecting saké for my restaurants is saké that customers can enjoy throughout the meal that will not interfere with the cuisine. Rice that is finely milled should brew into a graceful, pure saké, with an elegant, dry finish and without any off-flavors. Since NOBU restaurants are found on five continents with rich wine cultures, on the drink list we include a fruity saké that many customers will like. I've been fortunate to work with a brewery that can respond to all of my requests: Hokusetsu Shuzo brewery on the island of Sado in Niigata prefecture. Hokusetsu Shuzo brewery has all of the essential components for creating saké: excellent rice, pure water, clean air, and brewers who are passionate about their art.

Saké pairs naturally with sushi, for it distracts from some of the fishiness of the seafood, whereas wine will often emphasize this in fresh fish. Overseas, when I have guests who shy away from raw seafood, I encourage them to try it with saké, and often they are delighted at how delicious the paring is. Then they can enjoy their meal.

Chilled saké is not the only way to enjoy this beverage. Sushi rice is served at body temperature, and serving *junmai* saké warmed to about 100°F(38°C) is an outstanding partner. Hokusetsu's dry and lightly aromatic *junmai* saké will pair with any seafood. It enhances the taste of the sushi while highlighting the flavor of the saké for a great meal.

There are no rules when it comes to drinking saké. Just find a saké that you like. If you prefer a more aromatic saké like *daiginjō*, serve it chilled in a wine glass. Swirl the glass as you would with wine and enjoy its aroma. Saké can also be served in a brandy glass and warmed with your hands to help release its aromatics. When drinking it, let it warm up in your mouth and enjoy. These are just three ways to discover the allure of saké.

Twenty years ago, American-made saké was selling for three to four dollars a glass. When I began serving Hokusetsu saké at four times the price, my customers naturally were surprised. However, once they tried it, they could appreciate the difference. Currently Hokusetsu Shuzo brewery has a unique, upscale saké called YK35* which is now quite popular at many NOBU restaurants. I am thrilled to see that the saké is increasing both in quality and popularity around the world. I have much pride in Japanese saké.

*The Y is for Yamada Nishiki, the high-quality varietal of rice used; K stands for Kumamoto *kōbo* (yeast); and 35 indicates the amount of rice left after milling. It is rare that rice is milled this much, and it results in a very elegant saké.

Hokusetsu Shuzo brewery
http://sake-hokusetsu.com/

At NOBU saké and other Japansee liquors are used in several aperitifs. Most important is that the aperitif is a prologue to the cuisine that follows. Here are seven different cocktails that vary in design and flavor.

SAKÉ ROCK MOJITO

The refreshing combination of mint and lime is paired with an umami-rich saké that lingers on the palate.

SERVES 1

4 tablespoons Saké Rock
1 tablespoon lime juice
2 teaspoons simple sugar syrup
crushed ice
mint leaves

Saké Rock is a saké brand from Hokusetsu. It has a very high alcohol content for saké at 28 percent, because an amount of distilled alcohol is added during the brewing process. To substitute, use 3–4 parts *honjōzō* style saké to 1 part vodka.

Fill a highball glass with mint leaves and crushed ice. Combine Saké Rock, lime juice, and simple sugar syrup in a cocktail shaker. Shake until well mixed. Pour over the mint leaves and crushed ice in the glass and stir lightly. Garnish with mint leaves.

SAKÉ ROCK

With 28 percent alcohol, this original saké has a dry and strong finish, which makes it an excellent partner with food.

SERVES 1

Saké Rock (PAGE 136)
ice, preferably an ice ball
1 lemon wedge
salt flakes, such as Maldon or fleur de sel

Moisten half the rim of a rocks glass with a lemon wedge. Spread the salt flakes in a cooking tray. Dip the rim of the glass into the salt and roll until the wet rim is coated with salt.

Place the ice in the glass and pour in Saké Rock.

MATSUHISA MARTINI

As evident by the name, this is one of NOBU's signature cocktails. This full-flavored martini with aromas of *daiginjō* and vodka is enhanced with pickled ginger.

SERVES 1

4 tablespoons *daiginjō* saké
4 tablespoons vodka
2 to 3 slices *gari* pickled ginger, store-bought
ice
3 thin cucumber slices

Arrange the cucumber slices on the bottom of a martini glass.

Combine the saké, vodka, and *gari* pickled ginger with some ice in a cocktail shaker. Shake well until the ginger permeates the saké mixture. Pour the mixture through a strainer into the glass.

CHŌKOKUJI BOTAN

Red peony petals from the Chōkokuji temple on Sado Island are steeped in rice *shōchū,* a Japanese distilled spirit, producing a gorgeous shade of pink. The color and aroma are enhanced when served on the rocks.

SERVES 1

Chōkokuji Botan
1 strip lemon peel
1 to 2 large ice cubes

Chōkokuji Botan is a brand of sweet liquor from Hokusetsu Shuzo brewery.

Place the ice cubes in a rock glass and pour in Chōkokuji Botan. Garnish with lemon peel.

PLUM LIQUOR CHILCANO

The plum liquor (*uméshu*), made with rice *shōchū*, sugar, and fresh plums (*umé*), is rich with a nice finish. An ideal aperitif when paired with fresh ginger and lime to soften its sweetness.

SERVES 1

4 tablespoons plum liquor (*uméshu*)
ginger ale
grated ginger, to taste
2 lime slices
large ice cubes

Place the ice cubes in a highball glass and put the lime slices between the ice and the glass for a nice visual effect.

Pour in the plum liquor and ginger ale almost to the rim. Add grated ginger to taste and stir lightly.

PINK PEONY FIZZ

The aromas of berries make this cocktail popular with women. Low in alcohol, this is the perfect prologue to a meal.

SERVES 1

4 tablespoons Chōkokuji Botan (PAGE 138)
2 teaspoons raspberry-flavored syrup, store-bought
tonic water
2 blueberries
ice cubes
1 to 2 strips lemon peel

Place the blueberries and ice cubes in a highball glass.
Combine Chōkokuji Botan and raspberry syrup in a cocktail shaker and shake well. Pour into the glass. Add tonic water and stir lightly. Garnish with the lemon peel.

YUZU SAKÉ

Yuzu citron is renowned in Japan for its refreshing aroma, which is enhanced when partnered with an elegant *daiginjō* saké.

SERVES 1

4 tablespoons *daiginjō* saké
1 teaspoon *yuzu* juice
2 teaspoons *yuzu*-flavored syrup, store-bought
ice, preferably an ice ball

Place the ice in a rocks glass. Combine *daiginjō* saké, *yuzu* juice, and *yuzu*-flavored syrup in the glass and stir lightly.

SUSHI CO

Sushi makes a lovely meal in itself, or, when paired with other Japanese dishes, it becomes a course in a memorable meal. These popular dishes are from NOBU's full course sushi menu and perfect for a dinner party.

URSE DISHES

Sushi is often seen as an appetizer in the West, but rice is generally served as the last course before dessert in Japan, as it is at NOBU restaurants. Here is a taste of classic NOBU-Style dishes from his popular course menu with sushi.

PHOTOS FROM TOP TO BOTTOM:

MATSUHISA SHRIMP

WHITE FISH *TIRADITO* WITH *SHŌYU-JIO*

STEAMED MONKFISH LIVER PATÉ WITH MUSTARD VINEGAR MISO SAUCE

SUSHI COURSE DISHES

STEAMED MONKFISH LIVER PATÉ WITH MUSTARD VINEGAR MISO SAUCE

SERVES 4

7 to 10 ounces (200 to 300 grams) fresh monkfish liver
salt
Mustard Vinegar Miso Sauce (PAGE 151)
4 teaspoons caviar
baby green *shiso* leaves
4 *yamamomo* (red bayberry), optional

With the tip of a knife, remove all the blood vessels from the monkfish liver (PHOTO 1). Peel off the thin membrane that covers the liver and discard. Cut the liver diagonally into 2 to 3 thin pieces. Soak in 3% salted water (the basic ratio is 1 tablespoon salt to 2 cups/500 ml ice-cold water) for 30 minutes to 1 hour (PHOTO 2). Blot dry.

Lay a piece of liver on a sheet of plastic wrap. Tightly roll into a cylinder and twist both ends of the plastic. With a needle or a bamboo skewer poke holes into any air bubbles. Holding both twisted ends, press the cylinder against a working surface (PHOTO 3). Push and roll forward several times so that the cylinder will get shorter and thicker until it is 2 inches (5 cm) in diameter. Wrap the liver packet with a sheet of aluminum foil and twist both ends. Then wrap with a *makisu* and secure with a rubber band (PHOTO 4). Repeat with the remaining liver pieces.

Steam the *makisu-wrapped* liver packets in a steamer for about 40 minutes. Let cool at room temperature and then refrigerate until chilled and set.

Slice off 4 round pieces from the liver paté. Place Mustard Vinegar Miso Sauce on the bottom of the dish and top with the liver slices. Garnish with caviar, baby green *shiso* leaves, and *yamamomo*.

The remaining liver paté will keep up to 3 days refrigerated.

FIRST COURSE: *SHUKŌ* SMALL APPETIZERS

In Japanese *shukō* refers to saké-friendly small dishes that will make the saké more delicious. Fresh seafood is ideal in creating these *pinchos*, all signature Nobu dishes with his twist on these classic Japanese recipes. *Shōyu-Jio* (PAGE 169) garnishes white fish sashimi, Spicy Mayonnaise Sauce over broiled Matsuhisa Shrimp stuffed with green *shiso* leaves, and monkfish liver topped with caviar. (Recipes for the first two not included.)

143

SUSHI COURSE DISHES

SECOND COURSE: SASHIMI
SALMON NEW STYLE SASHIMI

New Style Sashimi is a signature NOBU-Style preparation. This partially cooked salmon dish with the aroma of sesame is popular with everybody, even with those who are not fond of raw fish. (See PAGE 26 for a similar recipe.)

THIRD COURSE: SALAD
SEARED SCALLOPS AND SPINACH SALAD WITH DRY MISO DRESSING

Salad greens are topped with flash-seared sashimi-quality scallops and dressed with aromatic and rich Dry Miso dressing.

SERVES 1

1 to 2 sashimi-grade scallops, each cut in half laterally
2 to 3 cups (1⅓ ounces/40 grams) baby spinach
2-inch (5-cm)-length Japanese leek (*naganégi*)
oil for deep-frying

Dry Miso Dressing
  1 teaspoon Dry Miso (see RIGHT)
  1 teaspoon *yuzu* juice
  1 tablespoon extra virgin olive oil
  1 teaspoon truffle oil
  2 teaspoons Parmesan cheese, freshly grated
  black pepper, freshly ground
1 teaspoon finely chopped red bell pepper
salt and pepper

Score the leek lengthwise. Remove the light green core and discard. Cut the leek in fine julienne strips along the fibers. Heat the oil to 325°F (160°C) and deep-fry the leeks for 3 to 4 minutes until browned.

Place the leek and baby spinach in a bowl, add the ingredients for the Dry Miso Dressing, and toss. Transfer to a serving bowl and garnish with red bell pepper.

Sprinkle salt and pepper on both sides of the scallops pieces. Sear over a *yakiami* grill or a grill for about 10 seconds on each side so that the outer surfaces are marked but the inner flesh remains uncooked. Arrange on the salad and serve.

DRY MISO
Spread a thin layer of smooth miso, which doesn't contain chunks of soybean, on a sheet of parchment paper. Dry in an oven at 160°F (70°C) for 12 hours. Break into fine powder with fingers and keep in an airtight container with a desiccant. It will keep until the expiration date of the miso.

SUSHI COURSE DISHES

FOURTH COURSE: SEAFOOD
MISO-MARINATED BLACK COD

This is one of Robert DeNiro's favorites and is now famous the world over as Nobu's signature dish. Rich in umami from the miso and with toasty notes, the grilled black cod is delectable.

SERVES 1

4 ounces (120 grams) fresh black cod (*gindara*)

scant 1 cup (200 ml) NOBU-Style Saikyō Miso (PAGE 151)

Dried Apricot Compote
- 5 to 6 dried apricots
- scant ½ cup (100 ml) water
- 2 tablespoons (25 grams) granulated sugar
- 1 teaspoon brandy

Yuzu Miso Sauce (PAGE 151)

hajikami pickled ginger, optional

Dried Apricot Compote: Combine all the ingredients for the Dried Apricot Compote in a saucepan. Bring to a boil, then lower the heat and cook until the apricots are soft. Remove from heat and let cool.

Blot any excess moisture off the black cod with a paper towel. Place the NOBU-Style Saikyō Miso in a container and add the black cod to marinate (PHOTO). Tightly cover and refrigerate for 4 days.

Remove the fish from the marinade and lightly scrape off the miso with your fingers. Place on a parchment paper on a baking pan and bake in an oven at 390°F (200°C) for about 10 minutes. Broil in an oven or a toaster oven if additional color is desired.

Arrange the fish and an apricot on a serving plate. Garnish with *hajikami* pickled ginger on the top of the fish. Squeeze a drop of *Yuzu* Miso Sauce on each corner of the plate. Serve immediately.

145

SUSHI COURSE DISHES

FIFTH COURSE: MEAT
GRILLED *WAGYŪ* BEEF WITH WASABI PEPPER SAUCE

This is a very popular meat dish at NOBU restaurants worldwide. Along with butter, garlic, and black pepper, the Wasabi Pepper Sauce is rich and aromatic, and not too hot, since some of the heat in the wasabi cooks out. There is no doubt that this sauce is wonderful with grilled *wagyū* beef.

SERVES 1

2½ ounces (75 grams) *wagyū* sirloin beef
1 broccoli floret
⅛ red bell pepper

Wasabi Pepper Sauce
½ teaspoon clarified butter (regular butter also works)
½ teaspoon grated garlic
4 teaspoons Wasabi Pepper Sauce Base (PAGE 151)
½ teaspoon black pepper

olive oil
saké
salt and pepper
oil for deep-frying

Place the broccoli floret on a baking pan. Season with olive oil, saké, salt, and pepper. Bake in an oven at 390°F (200°C) for 7 to 8 minutes. Cut the red bell pepper into bite-sized pieces. Heat the oil to 325°F (160°C) and deep-fry the pepper for 2 to 3 minutes.

Remove the beef from the refrigerator ahead of time to warm up to room temperature. Sprinkle with salt and pepper. Heat a grill over high heat and lightly grill the beef on the both sides. Transfer to a baking pan and cook in an oven at 450°F (230°C) for 3 to 5 minutes. Remove from the oven, cover the beef with aluminum foil, and let rest for about 5 minutes.

Wasabi Pepper Sauce: Make the sauce just before serving. Heat a saucepan with clarified butter and grated garlic until the butter is infused with garlic. Add the Wasabi Pepper Sauce Base and black pepper. Mix quickly to emulsify the sauce. Remove from heat as soon as it comes to a boil.

Slice the rested beef into bite-sized pieces and arrange on a serving plate with the broccoli and red bell pepper. Spoon the sauce down on one side of the dish. Serve immediately.

NOTE
Wagyū beef is the meat that is well-marbled with fat from specific breeds of Japanese cattle.

SIXTH COURSE: SUSHI
NIGIRI SUSHI, 5 KINDS

Sushi from super-fresh fish and well-prepared seafood are the main course of this meal. (See similar recipes in the NIGIRI SUSHI chapter.)

SIMMERED *ANAGO* EEL WITH *ANAGO* BROTH REDUCTION
VINEGARED *KOHADA*
MEDIUM-FATTY TUNA (*CHŪTORO*)
FLOUNDER
BOILED JAPANESE TIGER PRAWN

SEVENTH COURSE: DESSERT
DESSERT BENTO BOX

A selection of desserts is presented in a Japanese lacquered box. The baking of the chocolate soufflé is timed to the customer's pace so it can be served hot out of the oven. (Recipes not included.)

WARM CHOCOLATE SOUFFLÉ
VANILLA ICE CREAM WITH CRUMBLES
RASPBERRY SAUCE
SLICED FRUIT

CLASSIC TECHNIQUES

SOY-SIMMERED SHIITAKÉ MUSHROOMS

Dried shiitaké mushrooms are simmered in sweet soy stock until tender. Look for thick mushrooms, since these will become juicy as they soak up the liquid. Retain the umami-rich water used to rehydrate the mushrooms. Using this liquid for cooking the mushrooms is a classic Japanese technique.

MAKES 10 SIMMERED MUSHROOMS

10 dried shiitaké mushrooms
1 quart (1 liter) water
½ cup (120 ml) saké
½ cup (120 ml) mirin
4 tablespoons granulated sugar
4 tablespoons soy sauce

Place the dried shiitaké mushrooms in a bowl of water and soak overnight in a refrigerator (PHOTO 1). Remove the mushrooms from the water and reserve the soaking water. (It may need to be poured through a coffee filter to remove any sediment.) Trim off the stems and discard.

Place the mushrooms and 2 cups (500 ml) of the reserved soaking water in a saucepan. Bring to a boil over high heat, skim, and reduce the heat to low. Simmer until the mushrooms are tender. Add saké, mirin, sugar, and soy sauce (PHOTO 2). Simmer for 30 to 40 minutes, until the liquid is syrupy. It will keep for 3 days refrigerated.

BOILED JAPANESE TIGER PRAWN

When a prawn is boiled it will curl up. Straight prawns are needed for sushi, so they are skewered before boiling. Look for the freshest prawns, ideally ones that are still alive. Just heat until cooked through.

fresh Japanese tiger prawns (*kuruma ébi*), each 1 ounce (30 grams) or 8 inches (20 cm) long, head, shell and tail attached
salt

Remove the head of a prawn with your fingers. Holding the prawn with legs facing up, stick a bamboo skewer into the tail right behind the legs (PHOTO 1). Skewer the prawn through the body towards the head.

Bring 6 cups (1.5 liters) of water to a boil in a pot large enough to hold the skewered prawns. Add 1 tablespoon of salt (1% solution) to the pot and add the skewered prawns. The prawns will first sink to the bottom and then float. Remove the prawns from the water when they are about to sink again, after about 1 minute. To test that the prawns are cooked, twist the skewer. If it moves easily, it is not fully cooked yet and should be returned to the pot.

Immediately transfer cooked prawns to ice-cold water to cool (PHOTO 2). Drain, remove the skewer, and blot dry.

JULIENNED THIN OMELET

The Japanese name of this julienned omelet is *kinshi* (beautiful silk threads) *tamago* (eggs), because the thin strips cut from the very thin omelet look like bright-colored silk threads. Those strips are used to brighten up dishes like sushi bowls.

MAKES 2–4 SQUARE OR RECTANGULAR SHEETS

1 to 2 eggs

vegetable oil for frying

Crack the eggs into a bowl and beat gently. Try not to incorporate too much air. Strain the mixture through a fine-mesh strainer.

Heat a square or rectangular Japanese omelet pan over medium heat. Alternatively, a small round pan such as a crepe pan will also work. Take a small piece of paper towel, dip in vegetable oil, and lightly coat the entire surface of the pan with oil. Test the temperature by placing a small amount of egg mixture on the pan. It should cook immediately with a pleasant sizzling sound. Adjust the temperature if necessary by increasing the temperature or removing the pan from the heat as needed.

Pour in just enough of the egg to coat the bottom of the pan. Tilt and rotate the pan to spread the egg evenly into every corner. When the egg sets and its surface is almost dry, run chopsticks around the edges to loosen the omelet from the pan. Insert chopsticks under the omelet across its width, lift up, remove from the pan, and set on a plate (PHOTO 1). Repeat with the remaining egg, re-oiling the pan each time. Cut the thin omelet into fine julienne strips (PHOTO 2). It will keep for 2 days refrigerated.

THICK BAKED OMELET WITH FISH AND SHRIMP PASTE

Almost like a sponge cake, this omelet is noted for its sweet flavor and fluffiness. Grated raw mountain yam (*yamaimo*) and stiffly beaten egg whites give the omelet its airy texture. It is often served as the last item in a nigiri sushi course.

MAKES 1 LOAF, USING A 10×10×2-INCH (24.5×24.5×5-CM) SQUARE JAPANESE OMELET PAN AS A MOLD

10 eggs

2 egg whites, whipped to stiff peaks

generous 3 ounces (100 grams) peeled fresh shrimp

10 ounces (300 grams) fresh white fish paste, preferably *hamo* eel but other white fish such as cod or sea bream (*tai*) will also work

scant 1 cup (200 grams) sugar, preferably *wasanbon* sugar, but granulated sugar will also work

6 ounces (170 grams) mountain yam (*yamaimo*), preferably viscous Yamato variety, peeled and finely grated

2 tablespoons plus 2 teaspoons light-colored soy sauce (*usukuchi shōyu*)

2 tablespoons plus 2 teaspoons saké

⅓ cup (80 ml) mirin

salt

In a *suribachi* mortar, grind shrimp to a fine paste with a *surikogi* pestle. Add the fish paste, sugar, and mountain yam in that order. Mix and grind to a smooth paste. Add the light-colored soy sauce, saké, mirin, and salt. Mix in the beaten eggs little by little (PHOTO 1). Lightly fold in the egg whites with a rubber spatula (PHOTO 2). Alternatively, puree the shrimp in a food processor until completely smooth and add all the ingredients except the egg whites in sequence and blend well. Transfer to a bowl and lightly fold in the egg whites with a rubber spatula.

Cut a piece of parchment paper to fit and line the pan. Pour the egg mixture in the lined pan. To evenly spread and expel any air bubbles in the mixture, tap the mold a few times. (PHOTO 3)

Place in an oven at 325°F (160°C) and bake for 30 to 40 minutes. Check the progress by inserting a bamboo skewer in the omelet. If the skewer comes out clean, it is thoroughly cooked (PHOTO 4). Turn the omelet upside down on a wire baking rack. Remove the pan and the paper. Cool to room temperature. It will keep for 2 days refrigerated.

NOTE

If it is hard to find good fish paste, get fresh white fish fillets and puree in a food processor.

SOY-SIMMERED *KAMPYŌ*

Kampyō is a traditional Japanese ingredient. These long, ribbon-like strips of dried gourd are boiled before they are simmered in a sweet soy stock. Soy-Simmered *Kampyō* is often used for sushi rolls and sushi bowls.

MAKES ABOUT 3 CUPS
(17 OUNCES OR 500 GRAMS)

generous 3 ounces (100 grams) *kampyō* (dried gourd ribbons), preferably uncut

Simmering Liquid

2 cups (500 ml) Basic *Dashi* Stock (PAGE 113)
scant ½ cup (100 ml) soy sauce
scant ½ cup (100 ml) mirin
scant ½ cup (100 ml) saké
10 ounces (300 grams) granulated sugar

Wash the *kampyō* in cold water and drain. Bring a pot of water to a boil. Add the *kampyō* and boil for 30 minutes. The *kampyō* will expand, and it should be soft enough to leave an impression when pressed by a fingernail (PHOTO 1). Drain.

Combine the ingredients of the Simmering Liquid in a saucepan. Bring to a boil over high heat and add the *kampyō* (PHOTO 2). Lower the heat when it comes back to a boil and simmer for about 30 minutes (PHOTO 3). Remove the *kampyō* from the liquid and cool on a sieve (PHOTO 4). It will keep for 5 days refrigerated.

Reserve the simmering liquid for Simmered *Anago* Eel.

Using the Soy-Simmered *Kampyō* broth
SIMMERED *ANAGO* EEL

Simmered *Anago* Eel is used for all sushi categories. If you can find butterflied *anago* eel, then please try to make this. Be sure to thoroughly rinse off any slime to remove the eel's fishiness.

MAKES 5 SIMMERED *ANAGO* EELS

5 *anago* eels, generous 5 ounces (160 grams) each, cleaned and butterflied
coarse sea salt, as needed
about 3 cups (700 to 750 ml) reserved simmering liquid from Soy-Simmered *Kampyō* (see ABOVE)
1 tablespoon soy sauce
5 tablespoons granulated sugar

Place the *anago* eels in a bowl. Rub the skin well with some sea salt. Transfer one *anago* eel onto a cutting board, skin side up. Holding the tail with one hand, scrub the viscous slime off the skin with a scourer or a brush. This prevents it from having an unpleasant smell when it's cooked. Rinse off the salt with cold water. Repeat with the remaining *anago* eels.

Combine the simmering liquid from the Soy-Simmered *Kampyō*, soy sauce, and sugar in a saucepan. Bring to a rolling boil over high heat and submerge *anago* eels in the liquid one by one (PHOTO 1). Once all the fish are in the pan, bring back to a boil, then lower the heat and simmer for 10 minutes (PHOTO 2). Remove *anago* eels from the liquid and cool on a flat sieve or cooking tray (PHOTO 3). It will keep for 3 days refrigerated.

Using the Simmered *Anago* Eel broth
ANAGO BROTH REDUCTION

Simmered *anago* eel nigiri and octopus nigiri are traditionally glazed with a reduction sauce just before they are served (PHOTO 1). The broth used for simmering the *kampyō* and *anago* eels is reserved for making this reduction.

Boil the remaining liquid from the Simmered *Anago* Eel over high heat. Cook until the liquid becomes thick and has a glossy sheen, continuously stirring and scraping the bottom of the saucepan with a wooden spatula to prevent it from burning (PHOTO 2). Remove from heat just before it reaches the desired consistency, since it will thicken a bit as it cools. The sauce will keep for 2 to 3 weeks refrigerated.

NOBU SAUCES FOR SUSHI

Here are the essential NOBU sauces that are used for sushi. Thicker sauces are best stored in plastic squeeze bottles with small tips.

NOBU-STYLE SAIKYŌ MISO

MAKES ABOUT 4 CUPS (940 ML)

scant ⅔ cup (150 ml) saké
scant ⅔ cup (150 ml) mirin
1 cup (225 grams) granulated sugar
1⅔ cup (1 pound/375ml/450 grams) miso, preferably light brown, mild Shinshū miso

Combine the saké, mirin, and sugar in a saucepan. Bring to a boil over high heat and stir until the sugar is dissolved. Reduce the heat to low and add miso. Mix well with a whisk until the mixture is smooth, and then mix with a wooden spatula. Stir constantly until it comes to a boil. Remove from heat. Cool to room temperature before using. It will keep for 7 days refrigerated.

In the past it wasn't easy to obtain Saikyō miso outside of Japan, as is still the case for many parts of the world. Nobu created this miso mixture as a substitute for Saikyō Miso, with more readily available Shinshū miso.

MUSTARD VINEGAR MISO SAUCE

MAKES GENEROUS ⅔ CUP (170 ML)

1 teaspoon Japanese mustard powder
½ cup (125 ml) NOBU-Style Saikyō Miso
2 tablespoons plus 1 teaspoon rice vinegar

Mix the mustard powder well with 2 teaspoons of lukewarm water in a bowl to draw out the heat. Add NOBU-Style Saikyō Miso and rice vinegar. Mix well. It will keep for 7 days refrigerated.

YUZU MISO SAUCE

MAKES SCANT ⅔ CUP (150 ML)

½ cup (125 ml) NOBU-Style Saikyō Miso
½ tablespoon *Yuzu* or Lemon Puree
5 teaspoons rice vinegar

To make *Yuzu* Puree: Cut the *yuzu* in half and remove all the seeds. Puree the deseeded *yuzu*, peel and all, in a food processor.
Combine all the ingredients in a bowl and mix well. It will keep for 7 days refrigerated.

SPICY SAIKYŌ MISO SAUCE

MAKES GENEROUS ¾ CUP (190 ML)

⅓ cup (80 ml) NOBU-Style Saikyō Miso
⅓ cup (80 ml) *gochujang* (Korean sweet and spicy paste; store-bought)
2 tablespoons saké, brought to a boil and cooled

Mix together all the ingredients in a bowl. It will keep for 7 days refrigerated.

SPICY MAYONNAISE SAUCE

MAKES ABOUT 1 CUP (235 ML)

scant 1 cup (180 grams) mayonnaise
2 teaspoons Chinese chili garlic paste such as made by Lee Kum Kee (store-bought), a large batch pureed in a food processor or a small batch mashed in a bowl with the back of a spoon

Mix together the mayonnaise and Chinese chili garlic paste in a bowl. It will keep for 7 days refrigerated.

AVOCADO MAYONNAISE SAUCE

MAKES ABOUT ½ CUP (125 ML)

⅓ medium-sized avocado (1¾ ounces/50 grams)
¼ cup (50 grams) mayonnaise
1 teaspoon lemon juice

Mix together all the ingredients and puree in a food processor until completely smooth. It will keep for 2 days refrigerated.

YUZU SOY SAUCE

MAKES SCANT ½ CUP (110 ML)

5 tablespoons soy sauce
2 tablespoons + 1 teaspoon *yuzu* juice or lemon juice

Blend the soy sauce and *yuzu* juice in a bowl. It will keep for 5 days refrigerated.

GARLIC SOY SAUCE

MAKES GENEROUS ¾ CUP (205 ML)

6 tablespoons + 2 teaspoons soy sauce
6 tablespoons + 2 teaspoons saké, brought to a boil once and cooled
1 teaspoon grated garlic

Combine all the ingredients in a bowl. It will keep for 5 days refrigerated.

WASABI PEPPER SAUCE BASE

MAKES GENEROUS 1 CUP (260 ML)

3 tablespoons wasabi powder
2 tablespoons + 1 teaspoon cold water
2 tablespoons soy sauce
2 tablespoons reduced-sodium soy sauce
½ cup (120 ml) Basic *Dashi* Stock (PAGE 113)

Mix the wasabi powder with water. Add the remaining ingredients and mix. Mix again before using, since the wasabi may settle. It will keep for 3 days refrigerated.

NEW STYLE OIL

MAKES ABOUT ⅔ CUP (165 ML)

10 tablespoons olive oil
1 tablespoon roasted sesame oil (10% of olive oil)

Mix the oils in a bowl.

JALAPEÑO SALSA

MAKES ABOUT 1 CUP (250 ML)

generous 3 ounces (100 grams) red onion, finely chopped
1 jalapeño pepper, minced
2½ tablespoons lemon juice
1 tablespoon grape seed oil
½ teaspoon sea salt

Combine all the ingredients in a bowl and set aside for 10 to 15 minutes to let the flavors meld. It will keep for 3 days refrigerated.

CHARAQUITA SALSA

MAKES ABOUT 1⅔ CUP (400 ML)

generous 3 ounces (100 grams) onion, finely chopped
generous 3 ounces (100 grams) tomato, preferably a sweet and small Japanese variety, finely chopped
1 tablespoon + 1 teaspoon lemon juice
1 teaspoon salt

Combine all the ingredients and set aside for 10 to 15 minutes to let the flavors meld. It will keep for 3 days refrigerated.

CEVICHE SAUCE

MAKES ⅓ CUP (80 ML)

½ teaspoon sea salt
1½ teaspoons water
4 tablespoons lemon juice
2 teaspoons *yuzu* juice
1 teaspoon soy sauce
½ teaspoon minced garlic
½ teaspoon grated ginger
¼ teaspoon freshly ground black pepper
1 teaspoon *aji amarillo* chili* paste

Mix the sea salt and water in a bowl until the salt dissolves. Add the remaining ingredients and mix well. It will keep for 3 days refrigerated.

Aji amarillo is a South American hot yellow or orange chili pepper that is fruity with medium heat. It is sold as a paste at Latin grocery stores.

KNIVES FROM LEFT TO RIGHT:
USUBA-BŌCHŌ, YANAGIBA-BŌCHŌ,
MEDIUM-SIZED *DÉBA-BŌCHŌ*

BASIC SEAFOOD PREPARATION FOR SUSHI

While it is possible to make sushi from pre-cut sashimi or from a fillet (PAGE 14), if you are able to source fresh, sashimi-grade whole fish, then that is the ideal way to prepare it. The most important thing to remember when working with raw seafood is hygiene and sanitation (PAGE 14). While a *déba-bōchō* is ideal for cutting fish, sharp Western knives will also work.

FILLETING MACKEREL

The standard filleting method for a mackerel is a classic technique called *sanmai oroshi* in Japanese. This method results in two boneless filets and the skeleton. This technique can be used for mackerel, horse mackerel, sea bream, and other similarly shaped fish.

1 sashimi-grade mackerel, generous ⅔ to 1 pound

Scaling a Mackerel: Using a scaler or the tip of a knife, scrape away the scales of the mackerel in short strokes from the tail to the head. Be sure to double-check the area around the head, gills, and belly for scales. Wash well and blot dry.

Place the fish on a cutting board, with its head facing left and the belly facing you. Insert the knife right behind the pectoral fin at an angle, as shown, until the knife reaches the backbone (PHOTO 1).

Turn the fish over, with its head still facing left. Insert the knife in the same way, cut off the head, and discard (PHOTO 2).

Open up the belly from the head end. Scrape out the entrails with the knife and discard. Rinse off all the remaining organs and blood with water. Blot dry (PHOTO 3).

Make a slit from the belly to the tail along the backbone (PHOTO 4).

Rotate the fish so that its tail faces right and the back is towards you. Cut along the dorsal fin from the tail to the head, sliding above the rib bones (photo 5).

Carefully cut the upper fillet off the backbone with the tip of a knife (PHOTO 6).

Holding the tail with your left hand, as shown, insert the knife at the tail end and slide towards the head to free the upper fillet (PHOTO 7).

Insert the knife at the tail end and separate the fillet. Trim off the rib bones remaining at the belly (dark colored part) (PHOTO 8).

To make the other fillet, turn the fish over with its tail facing left and the back facing towards you. Cut along the dorsal fin from the head to the tail through the backbone. Rotate the fish so that its tail faces right, and cut from the tail to the head over the backbone. Free and separate the fillet in the same way as the other fillet.

153

BACK-CUT BUTTERFLIED *AJI*

Butterfly the fish into a single piece by first cutting into the back of the fish and removing the skeleton. The fish can be marinated in vinegar and put over sushi rice for a kind of box-pressed sushi, or soaked in salt water and air-dried, to be grilled later.

1 sashimi-grade *aji* (horse mackerel), 6 inches (15 cm) long

Remove the scales of the *aji*. See Scaling a Mackerel (PAGE 153).

Place the fish on a cutting board, with its head facing left and the back facing towards you. Insert the knife right behind the pectoral fin at an angle, as shown, until the knife reaches the backbone (PHOTO 1).

Turn the fish over, its head still facing left. Insert the knife in the same way (PHOTO 2).

Cut off the head and discard (PHOTO 3).

Turn the fish over with its tail facing left and the back facing towards you. Cut along the dorsal fin from the head to tail, sliding above the rib bones (PHOTO 4).

Cut until the very end through to the bottom of the belly, being careful to leave the belly (ventral) skin intact, but not through the skin. Butterfly the fish. Remove the entrails and discard. Rinse and blot dry (PHOTO 5).

Turn over the butterflied fish, with its tail facing right. Cut along the dorsal fin from the tail to the head above the rib bones and backbone (PHOTO 6).

Cut off the bones at the tail end and discard (PHOTO 7).

Remove the pin bones with tweezers (PHOTO 8).

BELLY-CUT BUTTERFLIED *SAYORI*

Butterfly the fish into a single piece by first cutting into the belly and removing the skeleton.

1 sashimi-grade *sayori* (halfbeak), 12 to 16 inches (30 to 40 cm) long

Remove the scales of the *sayori*. See Scaling a Mackerel (PAGE 153). Place on a cutting board, with its head facing left. Insert the knife right behind the pectoral fin, cut off the head, and discard (PHOTO 1).

Place the fish with its tail facing left and its belly facing towards you. Open up the belly from the head end (PHOTO 2).

Scrape out the entrails with the knife and discard. Rinse off all the remaining organs and blood. Blot dry (PHOTO 3).

Holding the flesh with your left hand, use tweezers to pull off the tough anal fins and the bones attached to them. Place the fish with its tail facing left and its belly facing towards you. Make a slit from the belly to the tail through the backbone. With the tip of a knife, scrape off the black-colored membrane attached to the inner flesh and discard (PHOTO 4).

Butterfly the fish and place on a cutting board with its skin side up. Insert the knife between the flesh and backbone from the head end, cut through towards the tail. Cut off the bone at the tail end and discard (PHOTO 5).

Trim off the rib bones on both sides and with tweezers remove the pin bones (PHOTO 6).

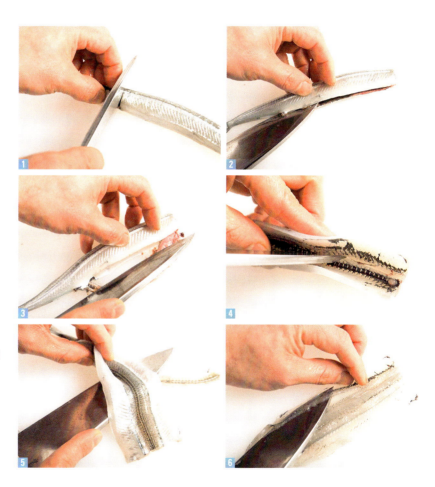

BACK-CUT BUTTERFLIED *MAMÉ AJI*

The head of this small fish becomes very tender and can be eaten after it has been marinated in vinegar. When butterflying this fish, be sure to leave the head on.

1 sashimi-grade *mamé aji* (baby horse mackerel), 3 to 4 inches (8 to 10 cm) long

Remove the scales of the *mamé aji*. See Scaling a Mackerel (PAGE 153) (PHOTO 1).

　Slice off the external spine-like scales, near the tail end, on both sides of the body (PHOTO 2).

　Place the fish on a cutting board, with its head facing right and the back facing towards you. Insert the knife along the dorsal fin from the head to the tail (PHOTO 3).

　Sliding the knife above the rib bones and backbone, butterfly the fish with its head attached (PHOTO 4).

　Remove the entrails and discard. Trim the rib bones with the tip of a knife (PHOTO 5).

　Turn over the butterflied fish, with its tail facing right. Cut along the dorsal fin from the tail to the head above the rib bones and backbone (PHOTO 6).

　Cut off the bones at the tail end (PHOTO 7).

　Remove the gills and eyeballs with tweezers and discard. Rinse well and blot dry (PHOTO 8).

156

BELLY-CUT HAND-BUTTERFLIED SARDINE

Since the flesh of the sardine is very delicate, it is very easy and quick to butterfly by simply using your fingers. Use a knife to cut off the head, open the belly, and remove the innards. Butterfly and pull out the skeleton using your fingers.

1 sashimi-grade sardine (*iwashi*), 6 to 7 inches (15 to 17 cm) long

Remove the scales of the sardine. See Scaling a Mackerel (PAGE 153) (PHOTO 1).

Place the fish on a cutting board, with its head facing left. Insert a knife right behind the pectoral fin and cut off the head (PHOTO 2).

Trim a portion of the belly, about 2 inches (5 cm), on a diagonal from the head end. Scrape out the entrails with the knife. Cut off the tail. Discard the entrails and tail. Rinse well and blot dry (PHOTO 3).

Place the fish on the cutting board with its tail end facing left and belly facing towards you. Cut along the backbone from the head to the tail end (PHOTO 4).

Butterfly the fish by gently opening it with your fingers (PHOTO 5).

Push your thumbs along the backbone to make it completely flat (PHOTO 6).

Pinch the end of the backbone with your left thumb and index finger and turn over the butterflied fish. Hold the backbone with your right thumb and index finger, and moving your right hand away, slide the flesh off the bone (PHOTO 7).

Trim off the rib bones on both sides of the butterflied sardine (PHOTO 8).

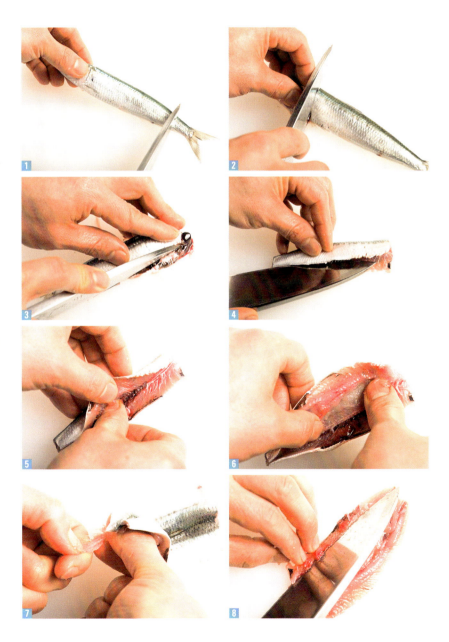

157

CLEANING OCTOPUS

1 medium size octopus, live
sea salt, as needed

Holding the head of the octopus with your left hand, insert the knife in the body cavity and cut the sinew that connects the body and the other parts (PHOTO 1).

Turn the head inside out. You have to do it quickly, since it moves a lot and will try to attach tentacles to your hands (PHOTO 2).

Cut off the entrails, ink sac, and egg sac if found. Discard the entrails and ink sac. Take care not to break the inc sac; it will make a mess if broken. Reserve the eggs if needed for another cooking purpose (PHOTOS 3, 4, 5).

Turn the head back to the normal position.

With the tip of a knife, cut off the mouth beak, which is at the bottom of the body. Discard (PHOTO 6).

Cut over the eyes and push out the eyeballs. Discard (PHOTO 7).

Place the octopus in a big *suribachi* mortar or a kitchen bowl and sprinkle with a handful of sea salt. Rub and knead with your hands in a similar motion as hand-washing a cloth. Rinse thoroughly with cold water after a slimy white foam develops. Repeat a couple of times until all of the sliminess is gone. This step prevents it from having an unpleasant odor when cooked (PHOTO 8).

CLEANING NORTH PACIFIC OCTOPUS

1 tentacle, sashimi-grade North Pacific octopus

Place the tentacle of the octopus on the cutting board. Insert the knife just underneath the row of suckers (PHOTOS 1, 2).

With a piece of paper towel or cloth, grab the skin with the suckers and gradually peel from the thickest end. Peel off the membrane as well. The skin with the suckers can be eaten if rubbed with salt to remove the sliminess and boiled (PHOTO 3).

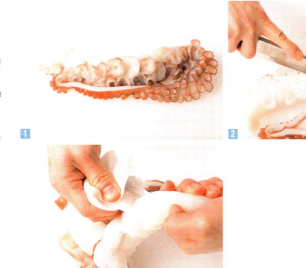

CLEANING SQUID

1 sashimi-grade squid, such as *surumé ika, yari ika, shiro ika*

Put your fingers in the body cavity of the squid to break the sinew that connects the body to the other parts (PHOTO 1).

Pull the tentacles along with the head and entrails out of the body. Take care not to break the black-colored ink sac; it will make a mess if broken. The tentacles and entrails can be reserved for another cooking purpose (PHOTO 2).

Put your fingers in the body cavity again and remove the soft and translucent bone attached to the inner surface of the body and discard.

With your fingers, hold the triangular fins of the squid and pull down to remove, so that some part of the skin will be peeled off as well. Using a piece of paper towel or cloth if needed, hold the remaining skin and continue to peel. Discard the skin. The triangular fins may be reserved for another cooking purpose (PHOTO 3).

Rinse and remove the entrails remaining in the body cavity. Blot dry.

Cut open the body along the line where the soft bone was. You will have a triangular sheet of squid. Peel away the inner membrane attached to the inner surface of the cavity (PHOTO 4).

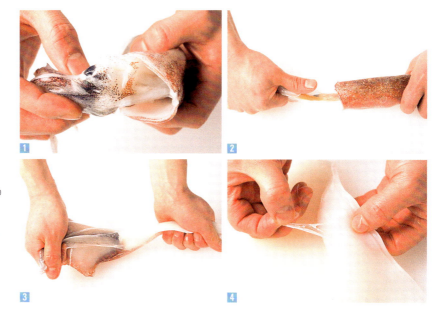

159

SHUCKING *AKAGAI* CLAMS

1 *akagai* clam, live

sea salt

Insert the tip of a small knife or a clam knife in the hinge of the *akagai* clam and twist to open the hinge. The shell is brittle and may break easily (PHOTO 1).

Insert the knife into the opening and force open. Cut through the 4 adductor muscle tissues that connect the clam and the shell. Remove the clam (PHOTO 2).

Separate and cut off the clam meat (orange-colored center part) from the outer mantle (PHOTO 3).

Clean the mantle by trimming the dark part and scraping off the sliminess with the tip of a knife (PHOTO 4).

Insert the knife laterally into the midpoint of the thickest part of the clam and butterfly the clam (PHOTO 5).

Trim off the brown-colored entrails from the both sides of the butterflied clam and discard (PHOTO 6).

Sprinkle some salt and lightly rub. Rinse with cold water and blot dry. You have to do it very quickly, since an *akagai* clam loses its freshness when in contact with water.

SHUCKING *HOKKIGAI* CLAMS

1 *hokkigai* clam, live

Insert a small knife or a clam knife into the opening of the *hokkigai* clam. Run the knife around the shell and force open (PHOTO 1).

Cut through the 4 adductor muscle tissues that connect the clam and the shell. Take out the clam (PHOTO 2).

Separate and cut off the clam meat from the outer mantle (PHOTO 3).

Bring a pan of water to a boil. Blanch the clam and the mantle for 5 to 6 seconds each (PHOTO 4).

As soon as the tip of the clam turns a reddish color, immediately transfer to ice water to cool. Wash well and remove any sliminess (PHOTO 5).

Insert the knife laterally into the midpoint of the thickest part of the clam and butterfly the clam (PHOTO 6).

Trim off the entrails from the both sides of the butterflied clam (PHOTO 7).

Clean the mantle by removing the brown parts and the membrane. Rinse with cold water and blot dry (PHOTO 8).

ABOUT THE CHEF AND THE RESTAURANTS

BIOGRAPHY

Nobu (Nobuyuki) Matsuhisa
Born in Saitama prefecture, north of Tokyo, in 1949

1967—After graduating from high school, Nobu took a live-in job at his first sushi restaurant in Tokyo, Matsuei Zushi. He worked at this restaurant for seven years and mastered the basic techniques of sushi and Japanese cuisine.

1973—At the age of 23 Nobu opened a sister shop of Matsuei Zushi in Lima, Peru, where he first came across dishes like ceviche and *tiradito*. Unable to find traditional Japanese ingredients in Peru, Nobu improvised with local ingredients, and here his unique, signature cuisine started to bloom. After two and a half years, Nobu moved to Argentina to work at a Japanese restaurant in Buenos Aires. After a year in Argentina he returned to Japan.

1977—Nobu opened the Japanese restaurant in Anchorage, Alaska. It was full from the opening day, but after only fifty days the restaurant was completely destroyed by a fire caused by a short circuit. Although he was in debt, a friend suggested that he move to Los Angeles, and there he worked as a sushi chef for nine years.

1987—Nobu opened a Japanese restaurant Matsuhisa in Beverly Hills. Using top-quality ingredients, making food from the heart, and making sure the customer was always satisfied was his philosophy, and Matsuhisa became a hot spot within a year of opening. Celebrities like Tom Cruise, Richard Gere, and Madonna soon became frequent customers. Nobu was serving Japanese cuisine that Americans found very appealing and easy to eat, and Matsuhisa eventually garnered the number-one ranking in the Zagat Survey, and the *New York Times* named it one of the top ten restaurants in the world. It was during this time that Nobu created his New Style Sashimi, rolls wrapped with thinly sliced *daikon*, and many other signature dishes.

1988—Robert DeNiro, a regular customer at Matsuhisa, asked Nobu to open a restaurant with him in New York City. Nobu declined this offer, since he was busy with Matsuhisa and was nervous about starting a new restaurant after what happened in Alaska.

1994—Robert DeNiro once more suggested that they open a restaurant together in New York City, and this time Nobu agreed. After four years of DeNiro's support and patience, Nobu was moved, and a partnership was born. Nobu was also ready to expand his business. NOBU New York City opens.

Thereafter

After that Nobu opened restaurants around the world, including London, Tokyo, Las Vegas, and more. In 2000, in partnership with Georgio Armani, together they open NOBU Milano to great fanfare and a warm welcome. Now Nobu's restaurants can be found on all five continents, and his first hotel, NOBU HOTEL, opened in Las Vegas in 2013. He served as the chef for the Golden Globe Awards consecutively in 2024 and 2025.

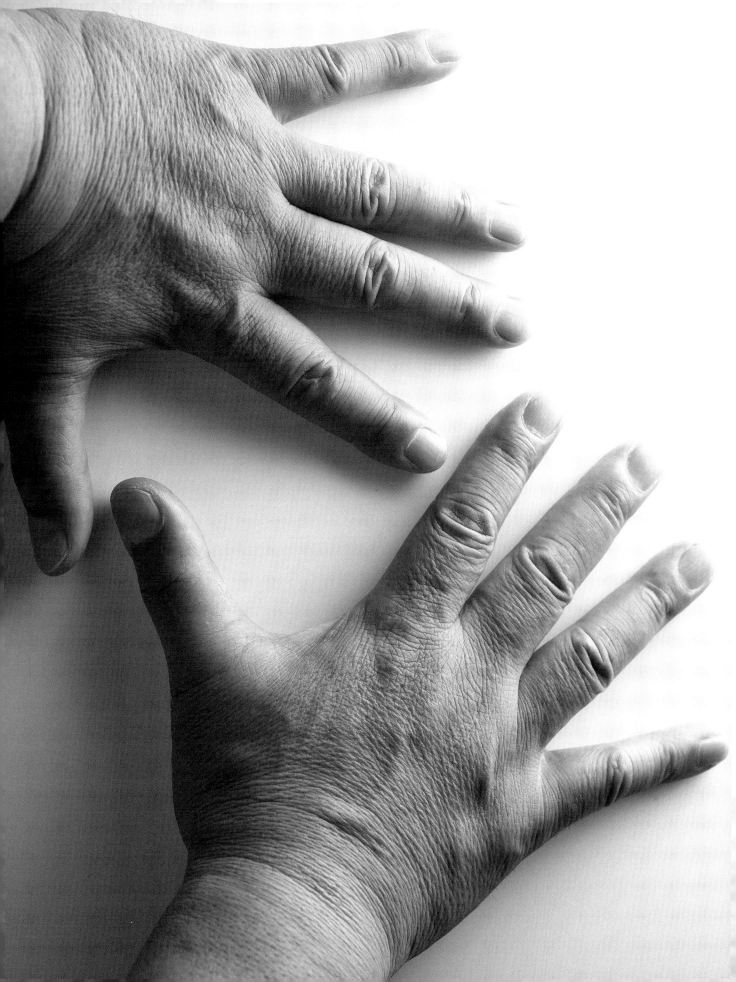

NOBU AND MATSUHISA RESTAURANTS

WWW.NOBURESTAURANTS.COM
H = Restaurant inside Nobu Hotel

NOBU

USA & CANADA

NOBU FIFTY SEVEN
New York, NY, U.S.A.

NOBU DOWNTOWN
New York, NY, U.S.A.

NOBU CAESARS ATLANTIC CITY H
Atlantic City, NJ, U.S.A.

NOBU WASHINGTON DC
Washington, DC, U.S.A.

NOBU ATLANTA H
Atlanta GA, U.S.A.

NOBU CHICAGO H
Chicago, IL, U.S.A.

NOBU MIAMI BEACH H
Miami Beach, FL, U.S.A.

NOBU NEW ORLEANS
New Orleans, Louisiana, U.S.A.

NOBU HOUSTON
Houston, TX, U.S.A.

NOBU DALLAS
Dallas, TX, U.S.A.

NOBU SCOTTSDALE
Scottsdale, AZ, U.S.A.

NOBU LAS VEGAS
at VARGIN HOTEL
Las Vegas, NV, U.S.A.

NOBU LAS VEGAS
CAESARS PALACE H
Las Vegas, NV, U.S.A.

NOBU LAS VEGAS AT PARIS HOTEL
Las Vegas, NV, U.S.A

NOBU PALO ALTO H
Palo Alto, CA, U.S.A.

NOBU MALIBU
Malibu, CA, U.S.A.

NOBU LOS ANGELES
West Hollywood, CA, U.S.A.

NOBU NEWPORT BEACH
Newport Beach, CA, U.S.A.

NOBU INDIAN WELLS
Indian Wells, CA, U.S.A

NOBU SAN DIEGO
San Diego, CA, U.S.A.

NOBU LANA'I
Lanai City HI, U.S.A.

NOBU TORONTO H
Toronto, Canada

ASIA PACIFIC

NOBU TOKYO
Tokyo, Japan

NOBU HONG KONG
Kowloon, Hong Kong

NOBU MANILA H
Manila, Philippines

NOBU KUALA LUMPUR
Kuala Lumpur, Malaysia

NOBU SINGAPORE
Singapore

NOBU BANGKOK
Bangkok, Thai

NOBU MELBOURNE
Melbourne, Australia

NOBU PERTH
Perth, Australia

NOBU SYDNEY
Sydney, Australia

MEXICO & CARIBBEAN

NOBU BAHAMA
Nassau, Bahamas

NOBU BARBUDA
Princess Diana Beach, Antigua and Barbuda

NOBU MEXICO CITY
Mexico City, Mexico

NOBU MEXICO CITY POLANCO
Polanco, Mexico

NOBU LOS CABOS H
Baja California, Mexico

MIDDLE EAST & AFRICA

NOBU CAPE TOWN
Cape Town, South Africa

NOBU DUBAI
Dubai, UAE

NOBU DUBAI by THE BEACH
Dubai, UAE

NOBU DOHA
Doha, Qatar

NOBU MARRAKECH H
Marrakech, Morocco

EUROPE

NOBU LONDON
London, England

NOBU LONDON SHOREDITCH H
London, England

NOBU LONDON
PORTMAN SQUARE H
London, England

NOBU WARSAW H
Warsaw, Poland

NOBU BUDAPEST
Budapest, Hungary

NOBU MILAN
Milan, Italy

NOBU MONTE CARLO
Monte Carlo, Monaco

NOBU BARCELONA H
Barcelona, Spain

NOBU IBIZA BAY H
Ibiza, Spain

NOBU MARBELLA H
Marbella, Spain

NOBU SAN SEBASTIAN H
Gipuzkoa, Spain

NOBU ISTANBUL
Istanbul, Turkey

NOBU SANTORINI H
Santorini, Greece

Matsuhisa

USA

MATSUHISA BEVERLY HILLS
Beverly Hills, CA, U.S.A

MATSUHISA ASPEN
Aspen, CO, U.S.A.

MATSUHISA VAIL
Vail, CO, U.S.A.

MATSUHISA DENVER
Denver, CO, U.S.A.

EUROPE

MATSUHISA PARIS
Paris, France

MATSUHI SAINT TROPEZ
Saint-Tropez, France

MATSUHISA VAL D'ISERE
Val-d'Isère, France

MATSUHISA MUNICH
Munich, Germany

MATSUHISA at BADRUTT'S PLACE
St. Moritz, Switzerland

MATSUHISA CALA DI VOLPE
Porto Cervo, Italy

MATSUHISA ATHENS
Athens, Greece

MATSUHISA MYKONOS
Mykonos Greece

MATSUHISA PAROS
Naousa, Greece

MATSUHISA LIMASSOL
Limassol, Cyprus

GLOSSARY

EQUIPMENT

Japanese omelet pan (*tamagoyaki nabé*)
Rectangular or square-shaped pan, 1–2 inches (2.5–5 cm) deep, used for making Japanese omelet, in a neatly rolled cylinder, a thin square or rectangular sheet, or in a sponge cake-like baked form. Different pan sizes determine the size of the omelet.

***oshi-zushi* box mold**
This wooden (or plastic) frame for making box-pressed sushi is a simple box with fitted top and bottom boards. Just place the sushi rice and fillings or toppings in the box, press, and you have box-pressed sushi.

***suribachi* mortar**
A *suribachi* is a Japanese mortar used with a *surikogi* pestle. The inside of the bowl is deeply grooved, which makes it effective for crushing or grinding nuts and seeds, mashing seafood, yam, tōfu, and so on. It is traditionally made of stoneware and should be heavy and sturdy.

***surikogi* pestle**
A wooden pestle used with a *suribachi* mortar to crush, grind, or mash ingredients. When selecting a *surikogi*, the ideal length should be twice as long as the diameter of the top of the *suribachi*.

***yakiami* grill**
Literally "grilling or broiling net," this is a handy Japanese kitchen tool to grill seafood, meat, or vegetables directly over a stovetop flame or an electric stovetop. It cannot be used with induction heat. It is a metallic grill, usually a square or rectangular, about 1 foot (30 cm) on each side. Sometimes there is a tray underneath the net to catch oil or other drippings while grilling. It may or may not have a handle. The grill may either be straight lines or a fine mesh; the fine mesh version is preferred, because small fish or delicate sushi toppings will not fall through when grilled.

FISH AND SEAFOOD

Seasonality is listed for Japanese seafood.

aji (horse mackerel) [June–Aug]
Trachurus japonicus. Typically 7 to 8 inches (20 cm) long, this small and silvery fish from the mackerel family has a simple but satisfying flavor. Popular as sashimi, marinated in vinegar, or grilled whole. **Mamé *aji*** (baby horse mackerel) are young *aji*, which are harvested in early spring and are never more than 4 inches (10 cm) long.

***akagai* clam** [Jan – Mar]
Ark shell; *Scapharca broughtonii*. An expensive sushi topping, the red-colored flesh has a sweet flavor and slightly chewy texture when it's fresh. Popular as sashimi, or it can be grilled.

***anago* eel** [Jul – Aug]
Conger myriaster. Also called conger eel, this tender eel is butterflied and simmered or grilled. Younger ones, 14 inches (35 cm) or smaller, are preferred for sushi in Japan. Butterflying eel is a highly skilled job, so it is best if you can find butterflied fillets to make Simmered *Anago* Eel (PAGE 150).

***asari* clam** [winter – early spring]
Japanese little neck clam; *Ruditapes philippinarum*. One of the most common clams in Japan, these small clams measure about 2 inches (5 cm) and are always cooked. Popular when steamed or cooked in soup, they produce a rich broth.

black cod (*gindara*)
Anoplopoma fimbria. Harvested in the North Pacific, this deep-sea fish can be up to 4 feet (120 cm) long. Rich in fat, black cod fillet is often marinated and grilled, as in NOBU's signature Miso-Marinated Black Cod (PAGE 145). Also known as sablefish.

flounder (*hiramé*) [Sep – Feb]
Paralichthys olivaceus. This large flatfish has a white flesh with mild flavor and delicate texture. It is popular as sashimi but also good cooked.

***hamo* eel** [Jun – Aug]
Pike conger; *Muraenesox cinereus*. This fierce eel has a very mild and delicate flavor, which is mostly appreciated in the west of Japan, especially in Kyoto. Not only used grilled or flash-blanched, the pureed meat can be the "hidden flavor" in Thick Baked Omelet with Fish and Shrimp Paste (PAGE 145).

***hokkigai* clam** [spring – summer]
Surf clam or hen clam; *Pseudocardium sachalinense*. Harvested in the cold waters of Japan and the Sea of Okhotsk, this large clam (4 inches/10 cm and larger) can be eaten

raw but is sweeter when cooked, such as sautéed, deep-fried, simmered, or blanched for topping sushi.

Japanese tiger prawn (*kuruma ébi*) [Sep – Nov]
Penaeus japonicus. Can be eaten raw if it's super fresh, but is often boiled for a sushi topping, grilled, or deep-fried as tempura. This prawn has a notable sweetness and umami, which comes out with its bright red color when cooked. Don't overcook it, since the flavor will fade and the texture becomes rubbery.

karasumi (dried mullet roe)
Also used in Italian cuisine, where it is called *bottarga*. The dark yellow, double-lobed sac of roe is salted and dried until it is very hard. It is sliced thinly or shaved and can be reminiscent of aged cheese. A gourmet treat in Japan often served with saké.

katsuobushi
Widely known as bonito, skipjack tuna (*Katsuwonus pelamis*) filets are steamed, dried, and smoked. Some are even fermented with a special mold and cured. The rock-hard filet is then shaved into delicate flakes. Rich in inosinic acid, *katsuobushi* is an essential component in *dashi* stock when combined with kombu. **Itogaki** (dried bonito threads) can be served over tōfu or vegetables or in sushi rolls.

kazunoko roe
Salt-cured herring roe in the sac is noted for its bright yellow color and crunchy texture. A unique version is **komochi kombu,** where the herring roe is laid on a piece of kelp by the herring in a thick layer, which is later harvested and cured. Both should be soaked in water overnight to reduce the salinity before being used.

kisu (sillago) [Jun – Sep]
Sillago japonica. This slender fish has a white, lean flesh with a fine texture. Often salt-grilled, deep-fried as tempura, or cured with kombu to obtain extra umami for sashimi or sushi.

kohada (gizzard shad) [Mar – May]
Konosirus pumctatus. *Kohada* is the name of younger *konoshiro*, which is consumed at 4 different stages of maturity in Japan. From the smallest, it's called *shinko* (less than 2 inches/4–5 cm), *kohada* (3–4 inches/7–10 cm), *nakazumi* (5 inches/12–13 cm), and *konoshiro* (6 inches/15 cm and up). In general, smaller is leaner, and all are usually vinegared. *Shinko* and *kohada* can be enjoyed for a very limited period each year and are very popular at sushi bars in Japan.

mackerel [Sep – Nov]
Saba; *Scomber japonicus*. Fatty and oily, this dark-blue and silvery fish is often salt-grilled or simmered in miso, but at the sushi counter it is commonly marinated in vinegar in a preparation called *shimé saba*. Mackerel loses its freshness very quickly, so confirm with the fishmonger if it's sashimi quality and then prepare it immediately.

masago roe
Capelin roe. Salted and red, this tiny roe is readily available in Western markets. It is slightly crunchy and popular as a sushi topping or filling. It can be substituted with *tobiko* (flying fish roe).

monkfish liver
Ankimo. Often referred to as "foie gras of the sea," the liver from monkfish (*ankō*; *Lophiomus setigerus*) is a popular dish in the winter. It is often steamed in and served with saké.

North Pacific octopus [Nov – Mar]
Hokkai-dako or *mizudako*; *Octopus dofleini*. One of the biggest octopi in the world, this can be eaten cooked or raw for its unique chewy texture. It is harvested in the cold waters of the Pacific Coast of Japan or North America.

octopus
Madako; *Octopus vulgaris*. The common octopus is boiled before being used as a topping for sushi. Most octopus is harvested in Africa. Carefully prepared octopus is not fishy and is tender and umami-rich when chewed.

sanma (Pacific saury) [Sep – Nov]
Cololabis saira. This long, silver-skinned fatty fish is popular when salt-grilled or simmered but is also a delicacy at the sushi counter either raw or marinated in vinegar.

sayori (halfbeak) [Mar – May]
Hyporhamphus sajori. The English name of the fish describes the unique mouth, where the lower beak is longer than the upper beak. This slender fish has a beautiful white flesh with a refined flavor and is served raw, poached in soup, or deep-fried as tempura.

sea bream (*tai*) [Mar – May]
Pagurus major. A very popular fish in Japan, sometimes called the "king of fish" for its beautiful appearance and delicate white meat. It can be served raw or cooked in a variety of methods.

shiro ika [spring – autumn]
Swordtip squid or white squid; *Loligo edulis*. Also called *kensaki ika*, this squid is umami-rich and has a distinct,

sweet flavor. Can be served raw, grilled, or as *himono* (sun-dried).

soft-shell crab
A crab, such as blue crab, Japanese blue crab, or swimming crab, that has just cast its exoskeleton and has a new soft shell, is generally called a soft-shell crab. Its shell is edible after the crab is deep-fried or pan-fried.

surumé ika [Jun – Aug]
Flying squid; *Todarodes pacificus*. The most common and available type of squid in Japan, the flesh has a chewy texture and is good for squid "noodles" or grilled or simmered.

tuna
There are four major varieties of tuna in the world: Pacific bluefin tuna (*hon-maguro* or *kuro maguro*, *Thunnus sorientalis*), bigeye tuna (*mebachi maguro*, *Thunnus obesus*), southern bluefin tuna (*minami maguro*, *Thunnus maccoyii*), and yellowfin tuna (*kihada maguro*, *Thunnus albacares*). All have different meat color and distinct flavors. A huge fish with deep red meat, Pacific blue fin tuna is the most popular and also expensive. **Medium-fatty tuna** (*chūtoro*) can be sourced only with the first three varieties.

unagi eel [Jun – Aug]
Freshwater eel; *guilla japonica*. This fatty eel is always cooked—normally butterflied, grilled, steamed, and glaze-grilled to make rich-flavored **kabayaki** (glaze-grilled *unagi* eel). Precooked and vacuum-packed *kabayaki* is sold frozen or in the refrigerator section at Japanese and Asian grocery stores.

yari ika [Dec – Mar]
Spear squid; *Loligo bleekeri*. This spear-shaped squid has a light taste and is available in winter in Japan. Served raw or cooked in a variety of methods.

yellowtail
Seriola quinqueradiata. Yellowtail is consumed at 5–6 different stages of maturity in Japan, and each stage has a name. Young yellowtail at 16 to 24 inches (40–60 cm) long is called **hamachi**; mature yellowtail at 32 inches (80 cm) or bigger is called **buri**. *Buri*, rich in fat, is usually wild; *hamachi* is commonly farmed and is available all-year long.

FRESH VEGETABLES AND HERBS

burdock root
Gobō in Japanese. This long, thin root vegetable has a stringy texture and woodsy flavor, which is appreciated. It often is sold with a little soil still clinging to it; it oxidizes quickly and discolors when peeled. Soaking in cold water minimizes this discoloration, though a certain amount of flavor will be released. Also see Pickled Burdock Root.

Chrysanthemum flowers
Yellow or a light lavender color, edible, fragrant fresh chrysanthemum flowers (*kikka*) are available only in autumn in Japan. The plucked petals can be quickly blanched and dressed or served raw over a salad. **Hoshigiku** are dried chrysanthemum petals and normally come to market in sheet form. Fresh petals are plucked and spread on flat mesh trays to be steamed and then dried.

daikon
Long, large Japanese white icicle radish has a crisp texture when eaten raw. Daikon is often grated or simmered and used as a garnish for sushi when finely julienned. It is available all-year round; sweet and juicy in the winter and sharp in the summer. Look for firm radishes.

énoki mushroom
Thin, long-stemmed white mushrooms with a tiny cap that can be consumed raw or cooked. Look for crisp mushrooms. Cut and discard the tough stem bottoms.

Japanese leek (*naganégi*)
This Japanese slender leek has mild flavor and finer fibers than European leeks. It is very aromatic when sautéed. When julienned, it should be scored lengthwise and the light green core removed because it's a little slimy and has a different flavor.

Japanese turnip (*kabu*)
Tender, juicy, and sweet, this white small turnip can be eaten raw or cooked. It is best in the middle of winter in Japan.

kaiwaré daikon sprouts
These sharp-flavored daikon sprouts are typically grown hydroponically. When raw or blanched they can be used to add some spice to sushi.

kinomé
Literally translated as "leaf buds of a tree," *kinomé* is the young sprigs of the *sanshō* (Japanese pepper; prickly ash) shrub, noted for its aromatic quality and gentle piquancy.

lotus root
Renkon or *hasu* in Japanese, the lotus root is planted and harvested in muddy bogs. It has many holes in cross-section because air pockets run the length of the sausage-like

rhizome links. It is crunchy when lightly cooked or sautéed and starchy when cooked for a long time or simmered. Soak peeled and cut lotus root in vinegar water to prevent it from discoloring.

mitsuba (trefoil)
Literary "three leaves," this delicate Japanese herb has a mild flavor and crisp texture. It should not be confused with cilantro/coriander.

mountain yam (yamaimo)
When grated, the paste is very viscous and slimy. It can be eaten raw or cooked and is often used as a thickening agent. The preferred variety for Thick Baked Omelet with Fish and Shrimp Paste (PAGE 149) is Yamato, a thicker or triangular-shaped yam. It is starchier and slimier than the cylinder-shaped common variety, but that also works.

myōga
Zingiber mioga. In the ginger family, this pink and purple flower bud is used for its fragrance and crunchy texture as a condiment or pickle.

shiitaké mushroom
This all-purpose, very earthy, brown mushroom with a large cap is used both in fresh and dried forms. Rich in umami (guanylic acid and glutamic acid), dried mushrooms are often simmered or used to make *dashi* stock, especially for vegetarian Buddhist temple cooking. Look for thicker and heavier mushrooms in both fresh and dried forms.

shiso
Perilla frutescens. In the mint and basil family, the *shiso* plant has a refreshing flavor and light mint aroma.

— **green *shiso***
A wide leaf with a serrated edge and is one of the most popular Japanese herbs. It can be served with any sashimi or sushi.

— **hana hojiso**
Flowering *shiso* stalk from the *shiso* plant. Most commonly the flowers are plucked at the table and eaten with sashimi or sushi.

— **hojiso**
Shiso stalk with seed pods from the *shiso* plant. Used in the same way as *hana hojiso* and enjoyed for its crunchy texture and cooling sensation.

wasabi
Wasabia japonica. Most often the root is peeled, grated, and served with sushi or sashimi. Look for fat and moist roots. Also, the **wasabi leaf** and stalk are edible and usually blanched to bring out their spiciness. Nobu also uses **wasabi powder** for a sauce. As with wasabi paste in tubes, which is widely available at Asian grocery stores, wasabi powder is normally processed from horseradish (*Armoracia rusticana*). The powder should be mixed with a small amount of water to make a spicy paste.

yuzu
Aromatic Japanese citron used for its fragrant skin and acidic juice. Look for bottled juice if fresh *yuzu* is not available.

DRIED OR PRESERVED FOODS, SEASONINGS AND DRINKS

azuki red beans
Red to maroon-colored small dried beans used in both savory dishes and traditional sweets. Since it infuses its distinctive flavor and bleeds a deep maroon when cooked in water, it is also used to tint other ingredients when cooked together.

Dry Miso
NOBU's original freeze-dried miso available at NOBU restaurants. The recipe for a homemade version is introduced on PAGE 144.

grain vinegar
Kokumotsusu in Japanese, this vinegar is made from a variety of grains and saké. It's good for marinating seafood.

Japanese mustard powder (karashiko)
Sharper than Western mustard, dark-yellow Japanese mustard comes as a powder or a paste. Nobu's recipe calls for powder as a purer product, which should be mixed into a stiff paste with small increments of lukewarm water to bring up its flavor and heat.

kampyō (dried gourd ribbons)
A long, 1/2-inch (1.5-cm) -wide ribbon-like strip is spirally shaved from a large gourd and dried. It should be boiled to soften before it is simmered.

katakuriko (potato starch)
A thickener, the modern version is made from potato, but the original version was from *katakuri* root (*Erythronium japonicum*). Cornstarch can be used as a substitute.

kōji
A type of mold (*Aspergillus oryzae*) used in the saké, miso, and pickling processes to help break down the starch in rice.

kombu
Laminaria japonica. Sold in dried form, kombu is a variety of kelp renowned for its natural glutamates, a source of umami. Most are named after the locations where they are harvested (**Rausu**, Rishiri, and Hidaka), or by its variety, like *ma* kombu; each variety has its own flavor and properties. At NOBU, high-glutamate Rausu kombu is preferred and is used not only for making *dashi* stock but also frequently for curing seafood and vegetables called for in the *kobu-jimé* technique. Look for thick sheets that are dark in color. The fine white bloom on the surface is a source of flavor, so it should not be wiped off.

kuzu starch
A thickening agent made from kudzu root. Compared to *katakuriko*, kuzu results in a silkier texture and is able to keep this texture even when cool, while other thickeners become watery.

mirin
An essential ingredient in Japanese cooking, mirin is a lightly alcoholic, syrupy liquid made from *mochigomé* sticky rice, rice *kōji* (PAGE 168), and a bit of *shōchū*. Mirin adds a rich flavor, sweetness, and a sheen to dishes. The best quality *hon mirin* ("true mirin") is made in almost the same process as that of saké brewing, and no sugar is added.

miso
A savory paste made from fermented soybeans, salt, and perhaps rice or barley. An essential ingredient in the Japanese pantry, it is used for soup, marinades, dressings, and more.

— **Hatchō miso**
Dark fudge-like miso made from soybeans only and aged for 2–3 years. It is rich in flavor. It is popular in the Nagoya region.

— **Saikyō miso**
Beige colored, naturally sweet miso from the Kyoto area that has a lower salt content than other misos. Nobu's original Saikyō miso is made based on Shinshū miso, because when he started working abroad it was still difficult to find authentic Saikyō miso outside of Japan.

— **Shinshū miso**
Most widely available, yellow to brown miso made with rice. It contains a medium amount of salt.

pickled burdock root
A thin and short burdock root is pickled in a soy sauce–based marinade. A popular pickle in Japan, it can give an earthy flavor and a crunchy texture to sushi rolls.

pickled ginger
— *gari* **pickled ginger**
Thinly sliced ginger lightly blanched in hot water then pickled in a sweet rice vinegar. It is served as a condiment or palate cleanser during a sushi course. It is naturally pale pink if young ginger (new crop) is used.

— *hajikami* **pickled ginger**
Pickled tiny young ginger with the stem attached is traditionally served with grilled fish. The name literally translates as "biting the end," for the root end of the stem is tender and can be eaten.

saké
Japanese brewed rice alcoholic beverage, used for drinking as well as for cooking. It is a tenderizer for proteins and adds umami to dishes. The grade of saké is determined by how much of the bran is milled away.

— *daiginjō* **saké**
at least 50% of a grain is milled away, and a bit of distilled spirit is added to make a fruity and aromatic saké

— *honjōzō* **saké**
a basic type of saké; at least 30% of the grain is milled away and a bit of distilled spirit is added

— *junmai* **saké**
pure rice saké with no distilled spirit added; at least 30% of the grain is milled away; usually richer in flavor and with a bit of acidity

Shōyu-Jio
Freeze-dried soy sauce. NOBU's original product available at NOBU restaurants.

soba
Buckwheat noodles, usually sold dried but recently sometimes sold fresh in the refrigerator section. Nobu suggests dried noodles for the recipe in this book.

soy sauce
Essential ingredient of the Japanese pantry made of soybeans, wheat, salt, and water. There are several types of soy sauce for different purposes in Japan, but in this book, if not particularly mentioned, regular soy sauce (*koikuchi shōyu*) is used.

— **light-colored soy sauce** (*usukuchi shōyu*) is saltier than regular soy sauce but lighter in color; it is used in light-colored dishes.

***wasanbon* sugar**
Artisanal-made, highly refined Japanese sugar, it can be substituted with granulated sugar.

INDEX

A

abalone, 105
aji (horse mackerel), 165. See also *mamé aji*
    butterflying, 154
    Vinegared *Aji* Nigiri, 76
aji amarillo chili. See chili, *aji amarillo*
Anago Broth Reduction, 150
    Nigiri Sushi, 5 Kinds, 147
    Simmered *Anago* Eel Nigiri, 88
akagai clam. See clam, *akagai*
anago eel. See eel, *anago*
appetizer sushi, 118-133
apricots, dried, 145
Arroz con Pollo (Rice with Chicken) in a Freeze-Dried Onion Cup, 128
asari clam. See clam, *asari*
asparagus
    Dragon Roll, 38
    Kombu-Cured Vegetables Sushi Bowl, 100
    Shrimp Tempura Roll, 32
    Spicy Rolls, 35
    Tuna and Asparagus Roll, 29
    Vegetable Roll, 23
avocado
    Avocado Mayonnaise Sauce, 151
    California Hand Roll, 45
    California Roll, 31
    Colorful Soy Sheet Hand Rolls, 48
    Dragon Roll, 38
    House Special Roll, 18
    Pickled Chinese Cabbage Roll, 43
    Salmon Skin Roll, 21
    Vegetable Roll, 23
    Vegetable Sushi, 124
Avocado Mayonnaise Sauce, 151
    Tuna and Asparagus Roll, 29
azuki red beans, 168
    Red Bean-Infused Octopus Nigiri, 84

B

baby horse mackerel. See *mamé aji*
baby sea bream
    Soup with Baby Sea Bream and Soba Noodles, 114
bamboo leaves, 94
bamboo shoot
    Sushi on Lettuce Cups, 126
    Traditional *Chirashi* Sushi Bowl, 106
Basic *Dashi* Stock, 113
    Clear Soup with Chrysanthemum Petals, 116
    Dashimaki Omelet with Sea Urchin Nigiri, 91
    Hakuni-Style Simmered *Anago* Eel Nigiri, 89
    Kaburamushi Turnip Soup, 117
    Red Miso Soup with Fruit Tomato, 115
    Soup with Baby Sea Bream and Soba Noodles, 114
    Soy-Simmered *Kampyō*, 150
    Traditional *Chirashi* Sushi Bowl, 106
    Wasabi Pepper Sauce Base, 151
beef, *wagyū*
    Grilled *Wagyū* Beef with Wasabi Pepper Sauce, 146
bell peppers
    Tricolored Sushi on Freeze-Dried Bell Pepper Shells, 129
bettara-zuké
    Vegetable Sushi, 124
black cod (*gindara*), 165
    Miso-Marinated Black Cod, 145
Black Spicy Roll, 35
black tiger shrimp. See shrimp, black tiger
blueberries
    Pink Peony Fizz, 139
Boiled Japanese Tiger Prawn, 148
    Boiled Prawn with Egg Yolk Crumbles Nigiri, 83
    Flash-Seared Seafood Sushi Bowl, 103
    New Year's Lucky *Futomaki* Roll, 37
    Nigiri Sushi, 5 Kinds, 147
    NOBU-Style Ceviche Sushi Bowl, 105
    Rainbow Roll, 41
    substituting, in recipe, 108
    Sushi Sandwich with *Monaka* Wafers, 130
Boiled Prawn with Egg Yolk Crumbles Nigiri, 83
bonito, dried. See *katsuobushi*
Box-Pressed Cucumber Sushi, 111
box-pressed sushi, 108-111, 165
Box-Pressed *Unagi* Eel Sushi, 108
burdock root, 167. See also pickled burdock root

Sushi on Lettuce Cups, 126
Traditional *Chirashi* Sushi Bowl, 106
buri. See yellowtail, *buri*

C

California Hand Roll, 45
California Roll, 31
carrots
    Kombu-Cured Vegetables Sushi Bowl, 100
    Salmon Skin Roll, 21
    Sushi on Lettuce Cups, 126
    Traditional *Chirashi* Sushi Bowl, 106
    Vegetable Roll, 23
    Vegetable Sushi, 124
caviar
    Gunkan Sushi with Three Toppings, 93
    Steamed Monkfish Liver Paté with Mustard Vinegar Miso, 143
ceviche, 105
Ceviche Sauce, 151
    NOBU-Style Ceviche Sushi Bowl, 105
Charaquita Salsa, 151
    Saké-Flavored Scallop Nigiri, 87
cherry blossoms, salt-preserved
    Soup with Baby Sea Bream and Soba Noodles, 114
chicken
    Arroz con Pollo (Rice with Chicken) in a Freeze-Dried Onion Cup, 128
    Sushi on Lettuce Cups, 126
    Traditional *Chirashi* Sushi Bowl, 106
chili, *aji amarillo*
    Ceviche Sauce, 151
chili, jalapeño
    Tricolored Sushi on Freeze-Dried Bell Pepper Shells, 129
    Yellowtail and Jalapeño Nigiri, 68
    Yellowtail and Jalapeño Roll, 29
chili powder
    Red Spicy Roll, 35
chili, *rocoto*
    Flounder Tiradito Nigiri, 63
Chinese cabbage (*hakusai*). See also pickled Chinese cabbage
    Vegetable Sushi, 124
Chinese chili garlic paste
    Spicy Mayonnaise Sauce, 151

Spicy Seafood Soup, 113
Chōkokuji Botan
    Chōkokuji Botan, 138
    Pink Peony Fizz, 139
chrysanthemum petals, fresh, 167
    Clear Soup with Chrysanthemum Petals, 116
    substituting in recipe, 108
chrysanthemum petals, dried (*hoshigiku*), 167
    Box-Pressed *Unagi* Eel Sushi, 108
chūtoro. See tuna, medium-fatty
clam, *akagai*, 165
    Flash-Seared Seafood Sushi Bowl, 103
    shucking, 160
clam, *asari*, 165
    preparation, 113
    Spicy Seafood Soup, 113
clam, *hokkigai*, 165
    Flash-Seared Hokkigai Clam Nigiri, 87
    shucking, 160,
classic techniques, 148-150
Clear Soup with Chrysanthemum Petals, 116
Colorful Soy Sheet Hand Rolls, 48
conger eel. See eels, *anago*
coriander
    Arroz con Pollo (Rice with Chicken) in a Freeze-Dried Onion Cup, 128
    Flounder *Tiradito* Nigiri, 63
    NOBU-Style Ceviche Sushi Bowl, 105
    Yellowtail and Jalapeño Roll, 29
crab, king
    Grilled King Crab Hand Roll, 46
crab, snow
    California Hand Roll, 45
    California Roll, 31
    Colorful Soy Sheet Hand Rolls, 49
    Flash-Seared Seafood Sushi Bowl, 103
    Gunkan Sushi with Three Toppings, 93
    House Special Roll, 18
    Kaburamushi Turnip Soup, 117
    New Year's Lucky *Futomaki* Roll, 37
    Pickled Chinese Cabbage Roll, 43
    Rainbow Roll, 41
crab, soft-shell, 167
    Soft-Shell Crab Roll, 21
Crispy Rice Cubes with Spicy Tuna, 120
cucumber, salt-wilted, 29
    Box-Pressed Cucumber Sushi, 111
    Salt-Wilted Cucumber Roll, 29
cutting fish fillets, 14

D

daiginjō saké. See saké, *daiginjō*
daikon, 167
    Flash-Seared Yellowtail Nigiri, 69
    Grilled King Crab Hand Roll, 46
    House Special Roll, 18
    Katsuramuki, 19
    Kombu-Cured Vegetables Sushi Bowl, 100
    Toro Rossa Roll, 25
dashi. See Basic *Dashi* Stock
Dashimaki Omelet with Sea Urchin Nigiri, 91
déba-bōchō, 15, 152
Dessert Bento Box, 147
Dragon Roll, 38
dressing
    Seared Scallops and Spinach Salad with Dry Miso Dressing, 144
drinks, 134-139
Dried Mullet Roe over Sea Bream Nigiri, 67
Dry Miso, 144, 168
    North Pacific Octopus Nigiri, 84
    Squid "Noodle" Nigiri, 80
    Tricolored Sushi on Freeze-Dried Bell Pepper Shells, 129

E

eel, *anago*, 165. See also Simmered *Anago* Eel
    Hakuni-Style Simmered *Anago* Eel Nigiri, 89
    Simmered *Anago* Eel, 150
eel, *hamo*, 165
    Thick Baked Omelet with Fish and Shrimp Paste, 149
eel, *unagi*, 167
    Box-Pressed *Unagi* Eel Sushi, 108
eggs
    Boiled Prawn with Egg Yolk Crumbles Nigiri, 83
    Dashimaki Omelet with Sea Urchin Nigiri, 91
    Julienned Thin Omelet, 149
    Thick Baked Omelet with Fish and Shrimp Paste, 91, 149
énoki mushroom. See mushroom, *énoki*

F

fish paste
    Thick Baked Omelet with Fish and Shrimp Paste, 91, 149
Flash-Blanched Squid Nigiri with Jalapeño Salsa, 81
Flash-Seared *Hokkigai* Clam Nigiri, 87
Flash-Seared Seafood Sushi Bowl, 103
Flash-Seared Yellowtail Nigiri, 69
flounder (*hiramé*), 165
    Flounder *Tiradito* Nigiri, 63
    House Special Roll, 18
    NOBU-Style Ceviche Sushi Bowl, 105
    slicing, 14
    Sushi with Pickled *Rakkyō* on Radicchio Boats, 127
Flounder *Tiradito* Nigiri, 63
freeze-dried bell peppers
    Tricolored Sushi on Freeze-Dried Bell Pepper Shells, 129
freeze-dried onions
    Arroz con Pollo (Rice with Chicken) in a Freeze-Dried Onion Cup, 128
freeze-dried vegetables, 128

G

Garlic Soy Sauce, 151
    Seared Tuna Nigiri, 60
    Toro Rossa Roll, 25
gari. See pickled ginger, *gari*
Germnon, 128
ginger. See also pickled ginger.
    hari shōga; "needle-cut ginger" 26, 70
    substituting, in recipe, 108
ginger ale
    Plum Liquor Chilicano, 138
ginkgo nuts
    Kaburamushi Turnip Soup, 117
    Traditional *Chirashi* Sushi Bowl, 106
glossary, 165-169
gochujang
    Spicy Saikyō Miso Sauce, 151
grapeseed oil, 132
Green Spicy Roll, 35
Grilled King Crab Hand Roll, 46
Grilled *Wagyū* Beef with Wasabi Pepper Sauce, 146
Gunkan Sushi with Three Toppings, 93

H

hajikami. See pickled ginger, *hajikami*
Hakuni-Style Simmered *Anago* Eel Nigiri, 89
hakusai. See Chinese cabbage
hamachi. See yellowtail, *hamachi*
hamo eel. See eel, *hamo*
hana hojiso, 168
    Kombu-Cured Vegetables Sushi Bowl, 100
hand rolls, 44-49
    basic rolling technique, 45

handai, 12, 15
hari shōga. See ginger
hikarimono, 75-79
hojiso, 168
    Red Miso Soup with Fruit Tomato, 115
hokkigai clam. See clam, *hokkigai*
Hokusetsu Shuzo brewery, 134
horse mackerel. See *aji; mamé aji*
horseradish
    Wasabi Leaf Wrapped Sushi, 132
House Special Roll, 18

I

inside-out rolls, 30-41
    basic rolling technique, 31
itogaki (dried bonito threads), 166. See also *katsuobushi*
    Salmon Skin Roll, 21

J

jalapeño chili. See chili, jalapeño
Jalapeño Salsa, 151
    Flash-Blanched Squid Nigiri with Jalapeño Salsa, 81
Japanese tiger prawn. See prawn, Japanese tiger
Julienned Thin Omelet, 149
    Flash-Seared Seafood Sushi Bowl, 103
    Sushi on Lettuce Cups, 126
    Traditional *Chirashi* Sushi Bowl, 106

K

Kaburamushi Turnip Soup, 117
kaiwaré daikon sprouts, 167
    Colorful Soy Sheet Hand Rolls, 48
    Salmon Skin Roll, 21
    Toro Rossa Roll, 25
    Vegetable Roll, 23
    Vegetable Sushi, 124
kampyō (dried gourd ribbons), 168
    Soy-Simmered *Kampyō*, 150
karasumi (dried mullet roe), 166
    Dried Mullet Roe over Sea Bream Nigiri, 67
katakuriko (potato starch), 168
katsuobushi, 166. See also *itogaki*
    Basic *Dashi* Stock, 113
    Katsuobushi and Kombu-Cured Flounder Nigiri, 64
Katsuobushi and Kombu-Cured Flounder Nigiri, 64
katsuramuki, 19, 18-25

kazunoko roe. See roe, *kazunoko*
king crab. See crab, king
Kinjirushi, 11
kinomé, 167
    Flash-Seared Seafood Sushi Bowl, 103
    Flash-Seared Yellowtail Nigiri, 69
    Kombu-Cured Vegetables Sushi Bowl, 100
    Sayori Nigiri, 77
kisu (sillago), 166
    Kombu-Cured *Kisu* Nigiri, 78
knives, Japanese, 15, 152
kobu-jimé (kombu-curing)
    Katsuobushi and Kombu-Cured Flounder Nigiri, 64
    Kombu-Cured *Kisu* Nigiri, 78
    Kombu-Cured Vegetables Sushi Bowl, 100
    reusing kombu sheets, 64, 100
    Vegetable Sushi, 124
kohada (gizzard shad), 166
    Vinegared *Kohada* Nigiri, 76
    Rainbow Roll, 41
kōji, 168
kombu, 10, 169
    Basic *Dashi* Stock, 113
    Katsuobushi and Kombu-Cured Flounder Nigiri, 64
    Kombu-Cured *Kisu* Nigiri, 78
    Kombu-Cured Vegetables Sushi Bowl, 100
    kombu-curing. See *kobu-jimé*
    Soup with Baby Sea Bream and Soba Noodles, 114
    Vegetable Sushi, 124
kombu, *komochi*, 166
    New Year's Lucky Futomaki Roll, 37
Kombu-Cured *Kisu* Nigiri, 78
Kombu-Cured Vegetables Sushi Bowl, 100
komochi kombu. See kombu, *komochi*
kuzu starch, 169
    Kaburamushi Turnip Soup, 117

L

leeks, Japanese (*naganégi*), 167
    Pickled *Nozawana* Roll, 43
    Seared Scallops and Spinach Salad with Dry Miso Dressing, 144
    Toro Rossa Roll, 25
lemon
    Lemon-Cured Salmon Nigiri, 73
    Lemon Hand Roll, 47

Lemon Hand Roll, 47
Lemon-Cured Salmon Nigiri, 73
lettuce, iceberg
    Sushi on Lettuce Cups, 126
lettuce, red leaf
    Toro Rossa Roll, 25
lotus root, 167
    Sushi on Lettuce Cups, 126
    Traditional *Chirashi* Sushi Bowl, 106
    Vegetable Sushi, 124

M

mackerel, 166. See also Vinegared Mackerel
    filleting, 153
    Vinegared Mackerel Nigiri, 75
makisu, 15
mamé aji (baby horse mackerel), 165
    butterflying, 156
    Vinegared *Mamé Aji* Nigiri, 77
masago. See roe, *masago*
Matsuhisa Martini, 137
Matsuhisa Shrimp, 143
medium-fatty tuna (*chūtoro*). See tuna
Mini Sushi Cups, 96
mint, 136
mirin, 10, 169
Miso-Marinated Black Cod, 145
miso, Hatchō, 169
    Red Miso Soup with Fruit Tomato, 115
miso, Saikyō, 169
miso, Shinshū, 169
    Mustard Vinegar Miso Sauce, 151
    NOBU-Style Saikyō Miso, 151
    Spicy Saikyō Miso Sauce, 151
    Yuzu Miso Sauce, 151
mitsuba (trefoil), 168
    Spicy Seafood Soup, 113
    Sushi on Lettuce Cups, 126
    Traditional *Chirashi* Sushi Bowl, 106
monaka wafers
    Sushi Sandwich with *Monaka* Wafers, 130
monkfish liver, 166
    Steamed Monkfish Liver Paté with Mustard Vinegar Miso Sauce, 143
mountain yam (*yamaimo*), 168
    Thick Baked Omelet with Fish and Shrimp Paste, 149
mushroom, énoki, 167
    Vegetable Sushi, 124
mushroom, shiitaké, dried, 168
    Soy-Simmered Shiitaké Mushrooms, 148

mustard powder, Japanese, 168
    Mustard Vinegar Miso Sauce, 151
Mustard Vinegar Miso Sauce, 151
    Steamed Monkfish Liver Paté with Mustard Vinegar Miso, 143
myōga, 168
    Box-Pressed Cucumber Sushi, 111
    Pickled *Nozawana* Roll, 43
    Salt-Wilted Cucumber Roll, 29

N

namigata slicing method, 84, 91
New Style Oil, 151
    New Style Sashimi Roll, 26
    Salmon New Style Sashimi Nigiri, 70
New Style Sashimi, 26, 27, 70, 144
New Style Sashimi Roll, 26
New Year's Lucky *Futomaki* Roll, 37
nigiri sushi, 54-93
    basic hand-forming technique, 56
    Nigiri Sushi, 5 Kinds, 147
    NOBU Hand Roll Sushi Party Box, 50
    NOBU-Style, 19, 27, 63, 105
    NOBU-Style Ceviche Sushi Bowl, 105
    NOBU-Style Saikyō Miso, 151
    Miso-Marinated Black Cod, 145
noodles. See soba
North Pacific Octopus Nigiri, 84
Nozawana Roll, 43
nozawana-zuké
    Nozawana Roll, 43

O

octopus 166
    cleaning, 158
    Red Bean-Infused Octopus Nigiri 84
    Spicy Seafood Soup, 113
octopus, North Pacific, 166
    cleaning, 159
    NOBU-Style Ceviche Sushi Bowl, 105
    North Pacific Octopus Nigiri, 84
okra
    Colorful Soy Sheet Hand Rolls, 48
    Vegetable Roll, 23
olive oil, 21, 46, 144, 146, 151
olive oil, extra virgin, 144
omelet. See Julienned Thin Omelet; Thick Baked Omelet with Fish and Shrimp Paste
omelet pan, Japanese (*tamagoyaki nabé*), 165
onions, 128, 151
onions, red, 105, 132, 151

onions, freeze-dried
    Arroz con Pollo (Rice with Chicken) in a Freeze-Dried Onion Cup, 128
oshi-zushi mold, 165

P

Pickled Chinese Cabbage Roll, 43
pickled burdock root, 169
    Colorful Soy Sheet Hand Rolls, 48
    Salmon Skin Roll, 21
    Vegetable Roll, 23
pickled Chinese cabbage (*hakusai*)
    Pickled Chinese Cabbage Roll, 43
pickled ginger, *gari*, 169
    Flash-Seared Seafood Sushi Bowl, 103
    Matsuhisa Martini, 137
    Pickled *Nozawana* Roll, 43
pickled ginger, *hajikami*, 169
    Miso-Marinated Black Cod, 145
pickled *rakkyō*, 127
    Sushi with Pickled *Rakkyō* on Radicchio Boats, 127
pike conger eel. See eel, *hamo*
Pink Peony Fizz, 139
Plum Liquor Chilcano, 138
plump rolls, 18-25
    basic rolling technique, 18
prawn, Japanese tiger, 166. See also Boiled Japanese Tiger Prawn
    Boiled Japanese Tiger Prawn, 148
    Matsuhisa Shrimp, 142

R

radicchio
    Sushi with Pickled *Rakkyō* on Radicchio Boats, 127
radish
    House Special Roll, 18
    katsuramuki, 19
    Kombu-Cured Vegetables Sushi Bowl, 100
    Vegetable Sushi, 124
Rainbow Roll, 41
rakkyō, 127
Red Bean-Infused Octopus Nigiri, 84
Red Miso Soup with Fruit Tomato, 115
rice, 8
    Sushi Rice, 12
    washing and cooking, 12
rice vinegar. See vinegar, rice
rock shrimp. See shrimp, rock
rocoto chili. See chili, *rocoto*

roe, *kazunoko*, 166
    New Year's Lucky *Futomaki* Roll, 37
roe, *masago*, 166
    Dragon Roll, 38
    House Special Roll, 18
    New Year's Lucky *Futomaki* Roll, 37
    Soft-Shell Crab Roll, 21
    Sushi Sandwich with *Monaka* Wafers, 130
roe, mullet, dried. See *karasumi*

S

saké, 134, 169
saké, *daiginjō*, 169
    Matsuhisa Martini, 137
    Yuzu Saké, 139
saké, *honjōzō*, 169
    Saké Rock Mojito, 136
Saké Rock, 137
Saké Rock Mojito, 136
Saké-Flavored Scallop Nigiri, 87
saku, 14, 59, 73
salmon, 27
    Black Spicy Roll, 35
    Dragon Roll, 38
    House Special Roll, 18
    Lemon-Cured Salmon Nigiri, 73
    NOBU-Style Ceviche Sushi Bowl, 105
    Rainbow Roll, 41
    Salmon New Style Sashimi Nigiri, 70
    slicing, 14
Salmon New Style Sashimi, 144
Salmon New Style Sashimi Nigiri, 70
Salmon Skin Roll, 21
salmon skin, smoked
    Salmon Skin Roll, 21
salsas
    Charaquita Salsa, 151
    Flash-Blanched Squid Nigiri with Jalapeño Salsa, 81
    Jalapeño Salsa, 151
    Saké-Flavored Scallop Nigiri, 87
salt, 10. See also salt flakes; *Shōyu-Jio*
    preparation for *asari* clam, 113
salt-curing
    Box-Pressed Cucumber Sushi, 111
    hikarimono, 75-77
    Salt-Cured Tuna Nigiri, 59
    Salt-Wilted Cucumber Roll, 29
Salt-Cured Tuna Nigiri, 59
salt flakes, 88, 137
Salt-Wilted Cucumber Roll, 29

sanma (Pacific saury), 166
    Vinegared *Sanma* Nigiri, 77
sardine (*iwashi*)
    butterflying, 157
    Vinegared Sardine Nigiri, 76
Sasamaki, Sushi in Bamboo Leaf Cones, 94
sauces, 151
sayori (halfbeak), 166
    butterflying, 155
    Sayori Nigiri, 77
Sayori Nigiri, 77
scallops, 27
    Flash-Seared Seafood Sushi Bowl, 103
    NOBU-Style Ceviche Sushi Bowl, 105
    Saké-Flavored Scallop Nigiri, 87
    Seared Scallops and Spinach Salad with Dry Miso Dressing, 144
    Spicy Seafood Soup, 113
sea bass (*suzuki*)
    House Special Roll, 18
    New Style Sashimi Roll, 26
    slicing, 14
    Sushi with Pickled *Rakkyō* on Radicchio Boats, 127
sea bream (*tai*), 166. See also baby sea bream
    Dried Mullet Roe over Sea Bream Nigiri, 67
    filleting, 153
    House Special Roll, 18
    Rainbow Roll, 41
    slicing, 14
    substituting, in recipes, 108, 127
sea urchin (*uni*)
    Dashimaki Omelet with Sea Urchin Nigiri, 91
    Gunkan Sushi with Three Toppings, 93
    Kaburamushi Turnip Soup, 117
Seared Tuna Nigiri, 60
sesame oil, 151
shamoji, 12, 15, 43
shiitaké mushroom. See mushroom, shiitaké
shiro ika, 166. See also squid
    cleaning, 159
shiso, green, 168
    Box-Pressed Cucumber Sushi, 111
    Colorful Soy Sheet Hand Rolls, 48
    Lemon-Cured Salmon Nigiri, 73
    Lemon Hand Roll, 47
    Pickled *Nozawana* Roll, 43
    Rainbow Roll, 41
    Salmon Skin Roll, 21

Soup with Baby Sea Bream and Soba Noodles, 114
    Steamed Monkfish Liver Paté with Mustard Vinegar Miso, 143
    substituting in recipe, 108
    Sushi "Bon-Bons", 123
    Sushi Sandwich with *Monaka* Wafers, 130
Shōyu-Jio, 169
    Flounder *Tiradito* Nigiri, 63
    Hakuni-Style Simmered *Anago* Eel Nigiri, 89
    Lemon Hand Roll, 47
    Sushi with Pickled *Rakkyō* on Radicchio Boats, 127
    White Fish *Tiradito* with *Shōyu-Jio*, 142
shrimp. See also prawn, Japanese tiger
    Kombu-Cured *Kisu* Nigiri, 78
    Spicy Seafood Soup, 113
    Thick Baked Omelet with Fish and Shrimp Paste, 91, 149
Shrimp Tempura Roll, 32
shrimp, black tiger
    Shrimp Tempura Roll, 32
shrimp, rock
    Colorful Soy Sheet Hand Rolls, 48
shrimp paste
    Thick Baked Omelet with Fish and Shrimp Paste, 91, 149
Shukō Three Small Appetizers, 142
Simmered *Anago* Eel, 150
    Anago Broth Reduction, 150
    Colorful Soy Sheet Hand Rolls, 49
    Flash-Seared Seafood Sushi Bowl, 103
    New Year's Lucky *Futomaki* Roll, 37
    Nigiri Sushi, 5 Kinds, 147
    Simmered *Anago* Eel Nigiri, 88
    substituting, in recipe, 108
Simmered *Anago* Eel Nigiri, 88
slicing fish fillets, 14
smoked salmon
    Salmon Skin Roll, 21
    substituting, in recipe, 108
smoked salmon skin
    Salmon Skin Roll, 21
snow crab. See crab, snow
soba, 169
    Soup with Baby Sea Bream and Soba Noodles, 114
soft-shell crab. See crab, soft-shell
Soft-Shell Crab Roll, 21
Soup with Baby Sea Bream and Soba Noodles, 114

soups, 112-117
soy sauce, light-colored (*usukuchi shōyu*), 169
soy sauce, 169. See also *Shōyu-Jio*
soy sheets, 48
Soy-Simmered *Kampyō*, 150
    New Year's Lucky *Futomaki* Roll, 37
    Sushi on Lettuce Cups, 126
    Sushi Sandwich with *Monaka* Wafers, 130
    Traditional *Chirashi* Sushi Bowl, 106
Soy-Simmered Shiitaké Mushrooms, 148
    New Year's Lucky Futomaki Roll, 37
    Sushi on Lettuce Cups, 126
    Sushi Sandwich with *Monaka* Wafers, 130
    Traditional *Chirashi* Sushi Bowl, 106
Spicy Mayonnaise Sauce, 151
    Colorful Soy Sheet Hand Rolls, 49
    Crispy Rice Cubes with Spicy Tuna, 120
    Matsuhisa Shrimp, 143
    Shrimp Tempura Roll, 32
    Spicy Rolls, 35
Spicy Rolls, 35
Spicy Saikyō Miso Sauce, 151
    Toro Rossa Roll, 25
Spicy Seafood Soup, 113
spinach, baby
    Seared Scallops and Spinach Salad with Dry Miso Dressing, 144
squid, 27. See also *shiro ika; surumé ika; yari ika*
    cleaning, 159
    Flash-Blanched Squid Nigiri with Jalapeño Salsa, 81
    Flash-Seared Seafood Sushi Bowl, 103
    Spicy Seafood Soup, 113
    Squid "Noodle" Nigiri, 80
Squid "Noodle" Nigiri, 80
Steamed Monkfish Liver Paté with Mustard Vinegar Miso Sauce, 143
stock. See Basic *Dashi* Stock
sugar, 10
    Lemon-Cured Salmon Nigiri, 73
sugar, *wasanbon*, 169
    Red Bean-Infused Octopus Nigiri, 84
    Thick Baked Omelet with Fish and Shrimp Paste, 149
suribachi mortar, 165
surikogi pestle, 165
surumé ika, 167. See also squid
Sushi "Bon-Bons", 123
sushi bowls and box-pressed sushi, 99-101
sushi course dishes, 140-147

Sushi on Lettuce Cups, 126
sushi party ideas, 94
Sushi Rice, 12
sushi rolls, 16-49
    hand rolls, 44-49
    inside-out rolls, 30-35
    other rolls, 38-43
    plump rolls, 18-25
    thick rolls, 36-37
    thin rolls, 26-29
Sushi Sandwich with *Monaka* Wafers, 130
Sushi with Pickled *Rakkyō* on Radicchio Boats, 127
syrup, raspberry-flavored
    Pink Peony Fizz, 139
syrup, simple sugar
    Saké Rock Mojito, 136
syrup, *yuzu*-flavored
    Yuzu Saké, 139

T

tempura, 32
Thick Baked Omelet with Fish and Shrimp Paste, 91, 149
    Sushi Sandwich with *Monaka* Wafers, 130
thick rolls, 37
thin rolls, 26-29
    basic rolling technique, 26
tiradito, 63
    Flounder *Tiradito* Nigiri, 63
tomato
    Charaquita Salsa, 151
    NOBU-Style Ceviche Sushi Bowl, 105
    Pickled *Nozawana* Roll, 43
    Red Miso Soup with Fruit Tomato, 115
Toro Rossa Roll, 25
Traditional *Chirashi* Sushi Bowl, 106
Tricolored Sushi on Freeze-Dried Bell Pepper Shells, 129
truffles, black
    Lemon-Cured Salmon Nigiri, 73
tuna, 167
    Crispy Rice Cubes with Spicy Tuna, 120
    Flash-Seared Seafood Sushi Bowl, 103
    Gunkan Sushi with Three Toppings, 93
    House Special Roll, 18
    Nigiri Sushi, 5 Kinds, 147
    Rainbow Roll, 41
    Salt-Cured Tuna Nigiri, 59
    Seared Tuna Nigiri, 60
    slicing, 14

Spicy Rolls, 35
    Tuna and Asparagus Roll, 29
tuna, medium-fatty (*chūtoro*), 167
    Gunkan Sushi with Three Toppings, 93
    Toro Rossa Roll, 25
Tuna and Asparagus Roll, 29
turnip, Japanese (*kabu*), 167
    Kaburamushi Turnip Soup, 117
    Kombu-Cured Vegetables Sushi Bowl, 100
    Vegetable Sushi, 124

U

unagi eel. See eel, *unagi*
uni. See sea urchin
usuba-bōchō, 15, 19, 152

V

Vanilla Ice Cream with Crumbles, 147
Vegetable Roll, 23
Vegetable Sushi, 124
vinegar-curing, 75-77
vinegar, grain, 75-77, 168
vinegar, rice, 10, 12, 75-77, 83, 151, 169
Vinegared *Aji* Nigiri, 76
Vinegared *Kohada* Nigiri, 76
Vinegared Mackerel, 75
    Flash-Seared Seafood Sushi Bowl, 103
    New Year's Lucky *Futomaki* Roll, 37
    substituting, in recipe, 108
    Sushi Sandwich with *Monaka* Wafers, 130
    Vinegared Mackerel Nigiri, 75
Vinegared Mackerel Nigiri, 75
Vinegared *Mamé Aji* Nigiri, 77
Vinegared *Sanma* Nigiri, 77
Vinegared Sardine Nigiri, 76
vodka
    Matsuhisa Martini, 137
    Saké Rock Mojito, 136

W

wagyū. See beef, *wagyū*
Warm Chocolate Soufflé, 147
wasabi, 11, 168
    Wasabi Pepper Sauce Base, 151
Wasabi Leaf-Wrapped Sushi, 132
Wasabi Pepper Sauce, 146
Wasabi Pepper Sauce Base, 151
    Grilled *Wagyū* Beef with Wasabi Pepper Sauce, 146
wasabi powder, 168

Wasabi Pepper Sauce Base, 151
White Fish *Tiradito* with *Shōyu-Jio*, 142

Y

yakiami grill, 165
yam, mountain (*yamaimo*). See mountain yam
yanagiba-bōchō, 15, 152. See also knife, Japanese
yari ika, 167. See also squid
Yellowtail and Jalapeño Nigiri, 68
Yellowtail and Jalapeño Roll, 29
yellowtail, *buri*, 167
    Flash-Seared Yellowtail Nigiri, 69
    slicing, 14
yellowtail, *hamachi*, 167
    Flash-Seared Seafood Sushi Bowl, 103
    House Special Roll, 18
    Red Spicy Roll, 35
    slicing, 14
    Yellowtail and Jalapeño Nigiri, 68
    Yellowtail and Jalapeño Roll, 29
yushimo, 81
yuzu, 168
    Colorful Soy Sheet Hand Rolls, 48
    Flounder *Tiradito* Nigiri, 63
    Miso-Marinated Black Cod, 145
    Seared Scallops and Spinach Salad with Dry Miso Dressing, 144
    Sushi on Lettuce Cups, 126
    Yuzu Miso Sauce, 151
    Yuzu Saké, 139
    Yuzu Soy Sauce, 151
Yuzu Miso Sauce, 151
    Miso-Marinated Black Cod, 145
Yuzu Saké, 139
Yuzu Soy Sauce, 151
    Flash-Seared Yellowtail Nigiri, 69
    New Style Sashimi Roll, 26
    Salmon New Style Sashimi Nigiri, 70
    Yellowtail and Jalapeño Nigiri, 68

Z

zucchini
    Kombu-Cured Vegetables Sushi Bowl, 100
    Vegetable Sushi, 124

PROJECT EDITING: Keiko Harada (Sekaibunkasha Inc.)
PHOTOGRAPHS: Eiichi Takahashi
ART DIRECTION AND DESIGN: Kazuhiko Miki (Ampersand works)
LAYOUT: Miyoko Hayashi (Ampersand works)
EDITING AND TRANSLATING: Hiroko Sasaki
COPY EDITING: Yukari Sakamoto
PROOFREADING: Kim Schuefftan

This book is a revised edition of NOBU THE SUSHI BOOK, featuring updated store information and a new cover design. There are no changes to the recipes (as of February 10, 2025).

NOBU THE SUSHI BOOK

発行日　2025 年 3 月 25 日　初版第 1 刷発行

著　者　　松久信幸
発行者　　岸 達朗
発　行　　株式会社世界文化社
　　　　　〒 102-8187
　　　　　東京都千代田区九段北 4-2-29
　　　　　電話　03-3262-5118（編集部）
　　　　　　　　03-3262-5115（販売部）

印刷・製本　大日本印刷株式会社

©Nobuyuki Matsuhisa, 2025. Printed in Japan
ISBN 978-4-418-25309-8

落丁・乱丁のある場合はお取り替えいたします。
定価はカバーに表示してあります。
無断転載・複写（コピー、スキャン、デジタル化等）を禁じます。
本書を代行業者等の第三者に依頼して複製する行為は、たとえ個人や家庭内での利用であっても認められていません。